California

A Captivating Guide to the History of California, California Gold Rush and 1906 San Francisco Earthquake

Free Bonus from Captivating History
(Available for a Limited time)

Hi History Lovers!

Now you have a chance to join our exclusive history list so you can get your first history ebook for free as well as discounts and a potential to get more history books for free! Simply visit the link below to join.

Captivatinghistory.com/ebook

Also, make sure to follow us on Facebook, Twitter and Youtube by searching for Captivating History.

Contents

PART 1: HISTORY OF CALIFORNIA 1

INTRODUCTION 2

CHAPTER 1 – EARLY HISTORY AND THE ARRIVAL OF
AMERICA'S FIRST PEOPLE (YEAR UNKNOWN–1542) 9

CHAPTER 2 – ORIGIN OF CALIFORNIA'S NAME AND THE
FIRST EUROPEAN EXPLORATION (1510-1602) 20

CHAPTER 3 – FIRST EUROPEAN SETTLEMENT AND CONTACT
WITH THE NATIVE POPULATION (1769-1821) 24

CHAPTER 4 – MEXICAN CALIFORNIA AND THE YEARS
BEFORE CALIFORNIA JOINED THE UNITED STATES OF
AMERICA (1821-1846) 32

CHAPTER 5 – THE MEXICAN-AMERICAN WAR AND THE
UNITED STATES' ACQUISITION OF CALIFORNIA (1846-1848) 37

CHAPTER 6 – THE CALIFORNIA GOLD RUSH (1848-1860) 42

CHAPTER 7 – CALIFORNIA DURING THE CIVIL WAR AND IN
THE FIRST FEW YEARS OF DEVELOPMENT (1860-1869) 49

CHAPTER 8 – CALIFORNIA POST CIVIL WAR UNTIL THE
END OF THE 19TH CENTURY (1865-1900) 56

CHAPTER 9 – CALIFORNIA IN THE 20TH CENTURY (1900-2000) .. 67

CHAPTER 10 – PRESENT-DAY CALIFORNIA (2000-2021) 91

CONCLUSION 93

PART 2: THE CALIFORNIA GOLD RUSH 95

INTRODUCTION 96

CHAPTER 1 - THE DISCOVERY OF GOLD 98

CHAPTER 2 - GOING TO CALIFORNIA 105

CHAPTER 3 - THE LABOR FORCE 113

CHAPTER 4 - WOMEN IN THE CALIFORNIA GOLD RUSH 122

CHAPTER 5 - THE GOLDEN STATE 129

CHAPTER 6 - THE SIGNIFICANCE OF THE CALIFORNIA
GOLD RUSH ON THE GLOBAL ECONOMY 134

CONCLUSION 138

PART 3: 1906 SAN FRANCISCO EARTHQUAKE 140

INTRODUCTION 141

CHAPTER 1 - THE EARTH SHIFTS 143

CHAPTER 2 - A CITY SHAKES 146

CHAPTER 3 - INFERNOS CONSUME 150

CHAPTER 4 - THE DYNAMITE SOLUTION 155

CHAPTER 5 - EYEWITNESSES TELL THEIR STORIES 158

CHAPTER 6 - TALES OF HEROISM AND HEARTBREAK 161

CHAPTER 7 - CRIME CURBED THROUGH VIOLENCE 164

CHAPTER 8 - "STRANGERS IN OUR OWN STREETS" 171

CHAPTER 9 - SWEET RELIEF AND LABORS OF MERCY 176

CHAPTER 10 - RISING FROM THE ASHES 184

CONCLUSION 187

HERE'S ANOTHER BOOK BY CAPTIVATING HISTORY
THAT YOU MIGHT LIKE 188

FREE BONUS FROM CAPTIVATING HISTORY (AVAILABLE
FOR A LIMITED TIME) 189

REFERENCES 190

Part 1: History of California

A Captivating Guide to the History of the Golden State, Starting from when Native Americans Dominated through European Exploration to the Present

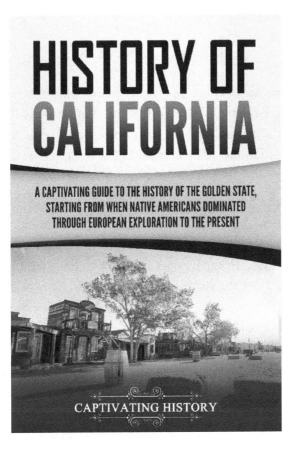

Introduction

Although California is known for its many landmarks, such as the Golden Gate Bridge and the Hollywood Sign, and its many famous personalities, it would take many centuries for the state to develop into what it is today, and it wouldn't actually be until 1850 that California was considered an American state at all.

California's earliest history actually dates back to many millennia ago, somewhere between 10,000 and 14,000 years ago. However, these years are far from exact, as it is still a matter of heavy debate amongst experts. Regardless of when the first settlers appeared, there is little debate as to how America's first people arrived. Thousands of years ago, hunters from Asia traveled along a land bridge that connected Asia to Alaska, known as the Bering Strait, while they pursued their prehistoric prey. Over time, these people made it to North America, where they gradually split up and spread out across the continent, eventually making it to California, likely by following the Pacific coast. Unlike the first people in Canada or other states in America, California's first people split off into hundreds and hundreds of smaller groups, as some wanted to settle while others continued to migrate. Over time, California's first people had established tribes all over the state. However, the groups had little contact with each other, which is yet another thing that sets

California's first settlers apart from the first settlers elsewhere in the country. This was mostly due to California's rugged landscape, which made traveling long distances less convenient than in other locations. In addition, the region's expansive wildlife and botany meant less migrating was necessary to find food. Seeing as the region of California is renowned for its diverse landscapes, including but not limited to the rainy redwood forests, Pacific Ocean coastline, the Mojave Desert, the snow-capped Sierra Nevada Mountains, the Central Valley fertile plains, as well as various smaller rivers, lakes, and microenvironments, every tribe quickly adapted their own culture, traditions, and lifestyle, which would have been dependent on their location. Overall, California's first settlers were quite peaceful, mostly since the groups had little contact, which allowed the tribes to truly establish their cultures and systems without violent interruptions. By the 16th century, California's first settlers, who had traveled together across the Bering Strait, split into more than 500 tribes spread throughout the region of California, with around 135 distinct unique dialects.

As the Native Americans in California established their cultures, the rest of the Americas were slowly being discovered over the course of the 15th and 16th centuries. Although the Spaniards would not actually make any moves to colonize California until the 18th century, California is believed to have received its name in the early 16th century. While there is some debate as to the true origin of the state's name, the most common origin story is that the name came from the fictional novel *Las Sergas de Esplandián* (*The Adventures of Esplandián*), written by Spanish author Garci Rodríguez de Montalvo. The romantic thriller was set on an island with sandy soil and hidden gold and riches. The island was located to the right of the Indies, referring to Southeast Asia. Although California is not an island and the Spaniards had no idea of the region's gold at the time, even before the Europeans first discovered California in 1542, they referred to the landmass north of Mexico as the island of California. As the Spaniards explored what would eventually become the Gulf of California, it was later discovered that California was, in fact, a peninsula attached to a far larger landmass. Over the course of the early 1500s, California would slowly be discovered as the Spaniards slowly explored and claimed the areas near their colony of Mexico; however, the region would remain completely untouched by the Europeans until the 1700s, leaving the Native Americans in California to continue to develop their culture and grow their population. It is estimated that by the 18th century, there were somewhere between 300,000 and 700,000 Native Americans in the region of California.

By the 18th century, while the United States of America had already begun its revolution, the Spaniards finally returned to California in order to explore and colonize the region that they had claimed centuries beforehand. The main reasons for Spain's renewed interest in California were that missionaries wanted to convert the region's native population and that Spain feared other countries might try to claim the land as their own, Russia being the primary threat, as they hunted otters in Alaska and began pursuing them down the Pacific coastline, just as the Native Americans had done millennia before. In 1769, Spanish explorers, led by Gaspar de Portolá, set sail from Mexico and began the journey of colonizing California. Though the route was hazardous and the maps were faulty, the boats finally reached California and arrived in present-day San Diego. Three months after arriving, Father Junípero Serra, who had been on one of the ships, created California's first mission, and he began making contact with the Native Americans so he could begin converting the tribes to Christianity. The tribes, who had lived uninterruptedly for thousands of years, establishing their own religions, cultures, and lifestyles, were given little choice, as they were often forced with violence to convert to Christianity. However, the missionary movement did not enforce only the Christian religion but also the European colonial way of living. The Native Americans would be forced to live in cramped walled enclosures even if they already had established villages nearby and were promptly taught Spanish along with many traditional European working skills, such as blacksmithing and brickmaking. Over the next thirty years, Mission San Diego would establish extensive European-inspired irrigation systems, which would aid the Native Americans in their forced labor of cultivating tens of thousands of acres. Although the Native Americans worked to cultivate the land and create a surplus of food, they reaped no rewards, as the food went to feed the European settlers. Any excess was exchanged with Mexico, allowing the Spaniards to acquire luxury items.

Over the next few years, Gaspar de Portolá and Junípero Serra continued to establish their presence in California; however, colonization did not really take place until after 1773. The small group who had arrived by boat in California was hardly enough to establish a European presence in the region, and the Spaniards in Mexico and Spain were not keen to embark on another long journey through the Pacific's hazardous waters to reach California. The land was not much safer either, and with California's deserts and rugged landscape, no European had managed to find a safe passage between Mexico and California, but that would change when the task was given to Juan Bautista de Anza. In 1774, with the help of the Native Americans, Anza discovered a safe path to California, and the next year, he led 240 men, women, and children, this time along with 700 horses and mules and around 350 cattle, to California, where they formed the city of San Francisco. The Spaniards had managed to create California's first real cities while at the same time reducing the Native American population by over 100,000 people. However, by the 19th century, California would no longer be theirs to colonize at all.

Just as the United States had gained its freedom from Britain in 1776, Mexico gained its independence from Spain in 1821, and while gaining its freedom, the newly created Republic of Mexico acquired California. Mexico promptly drove out the Spanish missionaries and parceled up the missionary land into land grants, which were known as ranchos. These land grants, given to a number of well-liked Mexican and Spanish civilians, created the first elite businessmen in California, which had previously been run by the church. Although the Native American population was freed from the missionaries, many of them ended up working as serfs on the Californian ranchos, their situation only mildly improved. Although the Mexican hold on California was way less strong than the Spanish church's was in the years before, Californians were not pleased with the new systems set in place by the Republic of Mexico, and public resentment started growing. During the period of Mexican California, the United States gradually increased its own interest in acquiring the region, and immigrants arrived from all over the country, which only added to the already growing Californian hostility toward Mexico. Following the 1846 Bear Flag Revolt, where a small group of Americans raised the first iteration of California's state flag and declared California's independence from Mexico, the United States and Mexico entered into war with each other over the state of California, among other issues. Finally, on February 2nd, 1848, the Mexican-American War ended, and California officially became a part of the United States, although they would have to wait to achieve statehood until they reached a minimum of 60,000 people.

At the end of the war, California had a fairly small population, and it seemed as if it could be at least a decade before California acquired statehood. However, they would blow past the 60,000 people requirement and achieve statehood in 1850. The reason for this incredible increase in population was the discovery of gold near present-day Sacramento, just as the Garci Rodríguez de Montalvo novel, *Las Sergas de Esplandián* (*The Adventures of Esplandián*), had predicted. Although the gold was discovered nine days before the end of the Mexican-American War, word would not actually reach the United States or the rest of the world until months later. However, Californians found out quite quickly, and they lined the hills near the river where the gold had been found with temporary tents and wooden huts. By 1849, the Gold Rush had officially begun, and people came from all over the world to try and strike it rich in California's gold mines. Over the course of 1849, it is estimated around 80,000 people, known as forty-niners, arrived in California. The following year, after some debates, California earned its statehood. The Gold Rush essentially birthed California's economy, as many who arrived in California pretty quickly realized that amongst all of the competition, one would actually be more successful if they set up businesses around the Gold Rush rather than mining for gold themselves. By the end of the Gold Rush, more than 300,000 people had permanently emigrated to California, which forced California to expand its cities and internal farming and manufacturing. As a result, a local economy developed quickly, and California became attractive to even those who were not interested in the Gold Rush at all.

The California Gold Rush would help fund the Union during the American Civil War, and by the end of the war, the United States realized the importance of its newly acquired state and the disadvantage of it not being connected to the rest of the United States. The end of the Civil War brought about the transcontinental railway, which, in turn, brought about another mass immigration to California. The expansion of Southern California, which at that point had remained mostly inhabited by the Native Americans, was also encouraged, and the new settlers promptly pushed the natives out of their land. By the end of the 19th century, California would be a diverse, multicultural society, with its own booming local economy and nothing but growth on the forefront.

By 1900, the population of California had grown to well over a million people, and the economy continued to flourish, even though almost all of the state's gold had been excavated at that point. New industries opened up every decade when the demands changed. For instance, California's suburbs grew with the automobile and oil industry boom, and California's weapon and aircraft manufacturing industries were born when the United States joined World War I. Although there were serious recessions, most notably the 1929 crash, which would bring about the Great Depression, California's economy always found a way to not only recover but also grow astronomically in the process. World War II would be, in many ways, a second gold rush for California, as millions would flock to the state for jobs.

Although the mass immigration to California was positive for the state's economy, it was not beneficial to all, especially in regards to the Native American population, who would be forced onto reservations, often in other states. As the population of California boomed, it quickly became one of the most multicultural states in the country, which was not without its own issues. While the white Americans prospered in California's economy, there was little upward mobility for foreigners or even racial minorities who had been citizens of California for decades at this point. With the growth of the economy came the growth of the divide between the rich and the poor that had started in Mexican California's rancho days. California would quickly become home to protests, rallies, and various social movements. Although the state had almost always been primarily Republican, by the end of the 20th century, California would become one of the most diverse, left-leaning, progressive states in the country, and by the 21st century, the protests, rallies, and various social movements over the years brought other openminded people to the state, transforming California into a major Democratic state.

Chapter 1 – Early History and the Arrival of America's First People (Year Unknown–1542)

In 1492, Italian explorer Christopher Columbus claimed the land he discovered in the Americas for Spain, but by this point in history, there were already many communities of people who inhabited the land and had done so for thousands of years. The first people of California were not Italian like Christopher Columbus nor Spaniards; in fact, they were not any type of European at all. Instead, they had come from Asia and traveled along a land bridge that no longer exists on the Arctic and Pacific Oceans. This ancient bridge, known as the Bering Strait, is believed to have been mostly grassy wetlands, but as water levels rose, the land was covered up by the water that connects Siberia to what is now Alaska. Regardless of whether the Bering Strait was land at the time or as it is now, a frozen bridge, the first people of America made quite a trip, seeing as the narrowest distance between mainland Russia and America today is around eighty-eight kilometers (fifty-five miles). What made this trip, which was done on foot, possible was the warmer climate and the access to food, and although historians are not too sure of the vegetation of the Bering Strait, the travelers had at least the meat of the prey they were hunting.

Although few experts debate that California's first people originated from Asia and arrived in America after hunting and following woolly mammoths, steppe bison, and other prehistoric mammals across the Bering Strait, when exactly they arrived is a point of contention amongst most historians and experts. The most common belief is that America's first people set foot in America sometime between 10,000 and 20,000 years ago and gradually spread across North America until eventually reaching what is now California, Baja California, and South America. However, a controversial discovery made at Cerutti Mastodon, a paleontological and archaeological site located in San Diego County, California, contradicts that common opinion. In 1992, during the construction of California's State Route 54, the team of construction workers manning the excavator dug up more than just dirt and rocks from the ground. The workers discovered large bone fragments on the site, which upon further digging also contained the skeleton of a mastodon, bone flakes, and several large stones. It is believed that the location was used by ancient humans sometime between 120,000 and 140,000 years ago as a "bone quarry," where the people would have used stone hammers to smash mastodon bones in order to use the material. This would, of course, place the first people in America over one hundred thousand years before the commonly believed date of their arrival. It took paleontologists and archaeologists until 2011 to actually place the date of the site, which was accomplished with the help of the trace amounts of uranium and thorium found within the mastodon bones. Seeing as it took the experts so long to date the site, and since the data is not entirely reliable, accurate, or foolproof, there is still much contention as to the actual date of arrival of America's first people. Many historians would rather stick to the more proven period between 10,000 and 20,000 years ago until further proof comes out saying otherwise.

Regardless of when the Asian settlers first stepped foot in America, it is known that the group began splitting into more distinct tribes and nations while gradually spreading throughout what is now Canada, the United States, and eventually South America. What makes the first people of California unique from the other native peoples of the Americas are the sheer number of different nations and tribes within the state, which all have their own unique culture, traditions, and lifestyle. This is due to California's diverse landscapes and habitats, which still exist within the state today. As the nations continued splitting up and spreading throughout California's vast land, they developed their own lifestyles based on the landscape around them. Some adapted sedentary agricultural lifestyles, while others were nomads and depended on hunting and gathering for sustenance. Since the small tribes became isolated in their unique environments, they developed their own distinct dialects, traditions, and cultures, which differed immensely from their closest neighbors. It is estimated that the original first people of America, who traveled together across the Bering Strait, split into more than 500 tribes spread throughout the state of California and gave birth to around 135 distinct unique dialects.

What greatly aided in solidifying the diversity of America's first people was California's rugged, difficult-to-traverse landscape, which isolated the individual tribes from one another. Although the nations were familiar with traveling rugged land, seeing as they had traversed much of the Pacific coast of North America by the time they had reached California, once the nations settled in their respective homes, they tended to stay within the area. Seeing as the state of California is ideal for various types of flora and fauna, there were far fewer nomad nations than in the rest of North America, and the tribes that were nomadic did not have to travel as far to find food. What this means is that there was far less interaction between the diverse tribes of California and that there was also little warfare, especially when compared to early tribes in other states. Overall, the first tribes of California experienced relatively peaceful lives, allowing them to develop more elaborate and complex systems and cultures than tribes undergoing destructive and distracting wars. The only outside interaction many of these people had was with neighboring tribes, who, due to proximity, likely shared some cultural commonalities. Of course, they also often engaged in the trade of goods and services with each other. These abnormally peaceful trading systems allowed California's first settlers to further diversify and develop their material objects. Seeing as California's tribes were so small and tight-knit, there was little need for strict political structures, unlike the larger nations in the rest of America.

Seeing as each individual nation developed in relative isolation, a tribe in the north of California would bear almost no cultural resemblances to a tribe in the south of California. That being said, seeing as an entire book can be written on any one of the distinctively unique tribes alone, grouping the hundreds and hundreds of tribes of California's early settlers into categories based on landscape and location will only allow for a small insight into the interesting cultures and diversity amongst the native Californians. Seeing as the neighboring tribes did share some cultural similarities, simply based on their shared landscape and communication, historians often group together California's tribes into the following categories: Northeastern tribes, Northwestern tribes, Central tribes, and Southern tribes.

Northeastern Tribes

Much like the rest of California, the landscape in northeastern California is extremely varied, and there are hundreds of different unique tribes that inhabit this region of the state. That being said, some of the more debatably "notable" tribes include the Modoc, Achumawi, and Atsugewi. The Achumawi or Achomawi tribes were located between Big Bend to Goose Lake, farther to the east in the northeastern region. The nation became known as river people, as their diet was extremely dependent on fishing, more so than other tribes. The Atsugewi tribes, who had trade relations and communication with the Achumawi tribes, resided mostly around Mount Shasta, which is one of the highest peaks in California. The group, as well as other tribes in the area, became known as the "Pit River Indians" due to the pits that were dug in and around the local creeks to make catching game easier. The Atsugewi and the Achumawi not only had trade connections but, seeing as their communities were located not too far away, also often had similar diets, which included berries, deer, rabbit, grass seeds, and tule. Many of the tribes in the eastern region of northeastern California also took advantage of the abundance of tule, which is an aquatic plant, by not only eating it but also lacing it together to create floor mats. The Modoc tribe, who today no longer inhabit California (as they have moved to Oregon and Oklahoma), may be one of the state's most well-known tribes due to the intense wars that would later happen against the United States military in the late 19th century. Prior to the arrival of Europeans, the Modoc tribe was scattered throughout northeastern California, seeing as they migrated seasonally to hunt and gather. During the winter months, they would stay sedentary in beehive-shaped, semi-underground lodgings built from wood and mud.

Of course, there were many more tribes who inhabited and still inhabit the northeastern region of California, including some who harvested obsidian for trade from the state's volcanic mountains. The obsidian was sharpened by any tribe who could get their hands on it to create ceremonial items, knives, hunting weapons, and, later on, weapons for war. Since volcanic glass is extremely sharp and strong, it became quite the sought-after commodity.

Northwestern Tribes

Similar to the northeastern region of California, there are many different landscapes, climates, and environments to the west that were inhabited by hundreds of tribes, each with its own distinctive culture and dialects. Some of the more well-known northwestern tribes include the Tolowa, Shasta, Karok, Yurok Hupa Whilikut,

Chilula, Chimarike, and Wiyot tribes, and similarly to the Modoc tribe out east, many of these nations were made known due to their involvement in what are known as the American Indian Wars in the late 19th century. Northwestern California is known for its redwood forests and the Pacific coast, as well as some mountains, lagoons, bays, rivers, and other waterways. Many of the northwestern tribes took advantage of the dense redwood forests at their disposal and used the lumber to build homes, which they constructed using a rectangular gabled design. Seeing as the tribes were taking down monstrous trees, which, when matured, have an average height of 200 to 240 feet, a lot of cutting was necessary to not only fell the massive trees but also to separate the lumber into manageable pieces. Since the tribes didn't have many of the effective tools we have today for taking down trees, they would actually burn the bases and then chop the tree down and split it up with elkhorn wedges. Although the tribes did traverse through the redwood forests on foot to cut down trees, their main way of travel and transport was by canoes, which they also built with the redwood lumber. Seeing as the northwest of California is littered with different waterways, many of which lead back to the Pacific Ocean, traveling by boat was the most efficient means of travel. The tribes of the northwest generally established their villages along the waterways, which made trade and relations between tribes more common than with those to the east, who were separated by rugged terrain.

The people who inhabited the northwest region of California suffered through many food deprivations and natural disasters, specifically earthquakes and floods, something that the people of California still deal with to this day. To ward off the many potential disasters that plagued the people inhabiting the region, many tribes had their own unique traditions, ceremonies, and rituals, which they practiced whether the community was lacking food or not. Furthermore, the northwestern tribes had their own unique artistry and craftsmanship traditions, which can best be seen in their basket making. The northwestern tribes are known for their twined baskets, which stand out against the baskets of other tribes who had access to different crafting materials. Another difference between the northwestern tribes and many other native nations of America is that the northwestern tribes had a clear hierarchy where lineage mattered, and those at the top would have more access to wealth, which, in their time, was the private ownership of bountiful food resources.

Central Tribes

Central California is a vaguely drawn-out large territory in the center of the state, which contains so many different landscapes, environments, and, of course, Native American nations. Some of the more well-known tribes who inhabit the Pacific coast, valleys, and mountain ranges in central California include the Pomo and Miwok nations, but, of course, these two barely scratch the surface. The Pomo tribe is well known today due to their coiled and twine baskets, which are elaborately designed with intricate color shifts and pattern work, which appear more like works of art than functional containers. The Pomo nation is also well known due to their proximity to what is now the city of San Francisco. The Pomo are known for their practice of the Kuksu religion, which is a Native American religion shared amongst a few northern and centralized nations in California. Traditionally, those who practice Kuksu have very specific ceremonies that are practiced to ensure good fortune in harvests, fertility, and other important matters.

The Miwok, who are spread all over central California, still has a larger population than most of the other nations in California. Within just the Miwok nation, there were seven distinct dialects and cultures, and by the time of European contact, the tribe had spread into over a hundred separate small villages. As with the rest of the Native Americans, even those outside California, every Miwok tribe established and developed their own unique customs and lifestyle based on where they were living, how many people were in the tribe, and other factors. The Miwok tribes located close to the coast lived in partially underground earth and pole-covered lodgings, and they gathered acorns, fished, and hunted deer and small game with bow and arrows. The Plains and Sierra Miwok, who were also known as the interior Miwok, lived in semi-subterranean earth-covered lodgings. When they hunted in the mountains, which they did in the warmer months, they would live in quickly assembled temporary lean-to lodgings. Like the Pomo nation, many of the interior Miwok tribes actively practiced Kuksu.

Although other tribes in the centralized region had their own systems and traditions, their general proximity in location means many of them shared some lifestyle elements. Whether in the mountains or on the coast, the tribes in central California were mostly hunter-gatherer groups who generally enjoyed an abundance of food such as acorns, deer, rabbit, elk, antelope, and salmon. Throughout central California, the semi-subterranean home was quite popular, although different tribes had different coverings depending on the available materials. Furthermore, the central tribes in the state were usually very spiritual. Religion was not limited to the followers of Kuksu, as many tribes had their own practices and customs to pray for good fortunes and to remember the patterns of renewal in the world and the circle of life.

Southern Tribes

Seeing as the territory of Southern California covers such a large expanse of land, with some of the most diverse environments in the whole state, including deserts and small islands, it is best to divide the region up into smaller sections to fully grasp the different tribes who settled here. In the north of Southern California, there are many tribes, including the Luiseno Cahuilla, the Kitanemuk, and, likely the most well-known tribe in California, the Chumash.

The Chumash are one of the most well-known nations in the state due to the fact that they were one of the first tribes that the Spaniards had contact with in the early 16th century. Although the Chumash people had a significantly larger population than many of the other tribes in California, some with over a thousand people, they were not as spread out as the similarly large Miwok tribes and instead were all centered around the Channel Islands. Since the tribe lived on various islands, they used double-oared canoes known as tomols, which were designed to carry hundreds if not thousands of pounds of goods and passengers. With their advantage of being surrounded by water and their art of constructing efficient boats, the Chumash often traveled to the other islands and to the main landmass to buy, sell, and trade using clamshell beads as a form of currency. The Chumash people were more than just skilled boat makers, for the tribe has also become known for their skilled artisans, who created wooden tools, intricate baskets, and soapstone sculptures. They established their villages on the water and lived in quite large dome-shaped homes, fashioned with many rooms that they shared with various members of their family. Seeing as the tribes lived on the water, one of their main sources of sustenance was fish, along with other sea animals. Like many of the tribes in California, the Chumash nation relied a great deal on gathering acorns. The reason acorns are not a commonly eaten nut today is due to the fact that they contain a lot of bitter tannins, which can be toxic if consumed in large amounts. However, the Chumash tribes found ways to leach the acorns of their bitter taste and toxicity and made them a staple in their diet. In contrast to their large populations of a thousand people or more in the Channel Islands, the Chumash communities in the desert in southeast California were often as small as 100 people.

The Cahuilla and Serrano were two separate groups that were spread throughout the south of the state, but both had villages in the Southern Californian deserts. To protect from extreme sun and heat, the people would build their homes in conical shapes with whatever materials they had native to their location, such as tule or arrow weed. Seeing as there was little European travel through the Californian desert, and since the desert native tribes were usually quite small, not much is known about the early people who established themselves in these harsh, hot conditions. That being said, traditions such as basket making, clay pottery, tattooing, sandstone carving, and more have been passed down through generations and give some indication as to how the early people might have lived.

Generally, it seems that the Southern Californian tribes shared many practices and systems, such as the naming of a chieftain, the belief in the village's shaman, and the separation of tribes into social classes.

The Native Americans before the Arrival of the Europeans

Although the United States' native population has been there for at least 10,000 years, some would say even 100,000 years, not much is known about their history for certain. Most of what we understand about America's first people comes from archaeological discoveries that line up with European historical accounts, current Native American traditions, and their history that has been passed down through word of mouth for generations. Although we attempted to summarize the Native Americans by geographical region in California, many of the villages that were near each other had very few similarities in customs, traditions, and rituals. After thousands of years of evolution and developing their own culture, they might as well have become a different race, and yet, seeing as they all arrived together, they are grouped together. The differences in lodgings perfectly demonstrate how differently the tribes lived. There were semi-subterranean earth-covered homes, dome-shaped dwellings, cone-shaped desert lodges, wood houses, large multi-room family homes, small nomadic hunting tents, and temporary lean-to homes. Some tribes traveled on foot, while others did so by boat. Unfortunately, most of the native tribes that are known today are only known due to their casinos, their mistreatment by the Europeans, and the wars with the Americans later in history. Yet, they had hundreds of unique cultures that existed far before Europeans claimed America. Upon the Spaniards' arrival in

California in 1542, there were around 130,000 Native Americans in what is now defined as the state of California, but so much is still unknown about the peoples that lived in the United States before the 16th-century arrival of the Europeans.

Chapter 2 – Origin of California's Name and the First European Exploration (1510–1602)

Eighteen years after Christopher Columbus sailed the Atlantic Ocean and set foot in the Americas in 1492, on what is now recognized as the Bahamas, and three years before Juan Ponce de León became the first European to set foot in the United States of America in 1513, California is believed to have received its name. Although there is some debate as to whether the true origin of California's name is, in fact, from the Native Americans or the Europeans, the most popular opinion is that the name originates from a fictional novel titled *Las Sergas de Esplandián* (*The Adventures of Esplandián.*) The romantic thriller, written by Spanish writer Garci Rodríguez de Montalvo, was published in 1510, some five years after the author's death, meaning the future name of the state was likely conceptualized many years before 1505. The novel follows the adventures of the mythical and beautiful Amazonian queen and warrior, Calafia, who, accompanied by her pet griffin, ruled over an island of woman. Garci Rodríguez de

Montalvo described Queen Calafia's island to have sandy soil and hidden gold and riches. This island paradise described in *Las Sergas de Esplandián* was named California. Whether the name truly originates from Garci Rodríguez de Montalvo's novel is, of course, unknown; however, it was the first written appearance of the name California, and seeing as the novel had been somewhat popular in Spain before the Spanish set foot in what would eventually become California, it makes sense that the name could have come from *Las Sergas de Esplandián*.

One year after Garci Rodríguez de Montalvo's novel was published, the Spanish explorer Vasco Núñez de Balboa became the first European to spot the Pacific shoreline. Although he did not technically set foot in California or anywhere on the Pacific coast, while exploring Panama in 1513, which the travelers reached from the Atlantic Ocean, Vasco Núñez de Balboa is said to have climbed a mountain and spotted the Pacific Ocean. The same year, the Spanish explorer Juan Ponce de León became the first European to set foot in the United States of America after settling in Puerto Rico and sailing to Florida.

In 1519, the Spaniards began their conquest of Mexico, and in 1521, Hernán Cortés officially defeated the Aztecs and succeeded in conquering Mexico. Following his conquest in Mexico, the Spaniard continued exploring both the Gulf of Mexico, which would lead him to Honduras, and the Pacific coast of Mexico. As he began aging, Hernán Cortés stopped leading expeditions and began commissioning other explorers to fulfill his curiosity. It would be one of his commissioned explorers, Francisco de Ulloa, who would lead the exploration of the Gulf of California, which he named the Sea of Cortés in 1539. Francisco de Ulloa's explorations in the late 1530s detailed that California was, in fact, a peninsula, although it would be years until this would be seen as a fact since it was still commonly believed that the land to the northwest of

Mexico was an island. During Francisco de Ulloa's expeditions, he also discovered the Colorado River.

In 1540, after Francisco de Ulloa's discovery, explorer Hernando de Alarcón was sent to sail the Colorado River. By this point, the Europeans were aware of Baja California, but it was not until Hernando de Alarcón's expedition that any European had seen Alta California, which refers to the upper region of the state. In the early 16th century, the explorers were still unsure as to whether California was an island or a peninsula, nor did they have any idea that the state was attached to a much larger continent. However, seeing as no one had actually set foot in California as of yet, the landmass was referred to as the island of California. In the summer of 1542, Spanish explorer Juan Rodríguez Cabrillo set off from the Mexican port of Navidad on an expedition through the Gulf of California (then the Sea of Cortés) to the Colorado River. Cabrillo and his crew are said to have first set foot in the state of California, which they named Alta California, on September 28th, 1542. They explored San Diego and the Monterey Bays, which made them the first Europeans to not only set foot in what is now the state of California but also the first to have contact with the native Californians. Juan Rodríguez Cabrillo estimated there were likely more than 100,000 Native Americans living in California upon his arrival in 1542.

Subsequent to Juan Rodríguez Cabrillo's official discovery of California, Spain began focusing on the exploration and colonization of the Philippines, which distracted them from further exploring California. Regardless of the Spanish Empire's plans in the Philippines, there was a general decline in Spanish explorations toward the end of the 16th century, which meant that California remained mostly untouched by the Europeans until the latter half of the 18th century. In 1602, Spanish explorer Sebastián Vizcaíno set sail from Mexico, alongside multiple vessels, to California, and after over half a year of travel, they reached San Diego. The city of San

Diego, which had been previously named San Miguel by Juan Rodríguez Cabrillo, was renamed San Diego by Sebastián Vizcaíno after the feast day of San Diego de Alcalá, which was to be celebrated two days after the group's arrival (the European feast is celebrated on November 12th). Sebastián Vizcaíno and his ships continued exploring, reaching Santa Catalina Island and sailing through the Santa Barbara Channel until entering the harbor at Carmel Bay. Although Sebastián Vizcaíno did not technically explore much more than Juan Rodríguez Cabrillo had many decades before, Vizcaíno named some of California's ports and cities (mostly after religious names or after his Spanish leadership) and helped to draw up much more accurate maps than what the Europeans were previously using, which would be depended upon until the late 18th century.

Chapter 3 – First European Settlement and Contact with the Native Population (1769–1821)

California before the Arrival of the Spanish in 1769

What would later become the state of California remained completely untouched by the Europeans for the next century and a half, which allowed the Native American population to grow and their culture to develop uninterrupted. From later mission records, archaeological records of villages, and various censuses conducted over the years, historians estimate the native population in California before the return of the Spaniards in the latter half of the 18th century was somewhere between 130,000 and 1,500,000. Seeing as the native population in California was so spread out, it is impossible to determine an exact number; however, the most specific estimation is that the native population was somewhere between 300,000 and 700,000.

Just before the Europeans set off to once again explore and colonize California, the rest of the United States of America, which then only included thirteen colonies located along the eastern seaboard, were about to head into the revolutionary era. In 1765, the British Parliament attempted to enact the Stamp Act, which was supposed to raise tax costs on stamps in order to raise the monarchy's revenue. The colonies were far from pleased by this new act and began protesting, rioting, burning stamps, and refusing to use stamps at all. There was much that went behind what set off the American Revolutionary War, but the fact the colonists had no representation in British Parliament is considered one of the prime issues. The American Revolution would officially begin in 1775. However, as the American revolutionaries began to defend their freedoms from British rule, California was only just being discovered and colonized. One of the reasons for the renewed Spanish interest in exploring California after leaving it untouched for over a century was that missionaries had been impatiently waiting and pushing to begin converting the Native Americans. Spain was also encouraged to return to California due to the European demand for sea otter pelts, which were originally found in the Alaskan Aleutian Islands but were hunted and driven south by the Russians. The third reason behind the sudden decision to resume exploration of California was the search for the Northwest Passage, a sea route that connected the Atlantic Ocean to the Pacific Ocean (this wouldn't be discovered by Europeans until the 19th century, though).

The Spaniards Set Sail in 1769

In 1769, Spain's viceroy sent explorers, which were to be led by Gaspar de Portolá, to begin the colonization of California. Gaspar de Portolá, a Spanish nobleman and soldier who was appointed governor of Las Californias in 1767, was instructed to set up bases in Alta California after being ordered to expel the Jesuits from Baja California. Three ships departed under Gaspar de Portolá's lead on their way to California. Seeing as the group was using faulty maps drawn up by Sebastián Vizcaíno in 1602, the voyage was far from peaceful. The group not only dealt with navigational errors that put them months off their route but also heavy winds and storms that they had not been expecting. Many of the men on the ships fell ill and died, and an entire boat of supplies was lost at sea. However, after months of difficulties, on April 11ᵗʰ, the first ship of men arrived in San Diego. On that ship was Father Junípero Serra, who would lead the Christian missionary movement in California over the subsequent years. Junípero Serra, who was later beatified, had entered the Franciscan Order in 1730, and after many years of teaching philosophy, he boarded a ship to Mexico in 1750 and was heavily involved in the missionary movement in Mexico until 1767. After embarking on the expedition led by Gaspar de Portolá, Father Junípero Serra arrived in California, eager to make contact with the Native Americans so he could begin converting the nations to Christianity.

Europeans Arrive in California

On July 16ᵗʰ, 1769, only three months after arriving in San Diego, Junípero Serra established Mission San Diego. Although the Native Americans who inhabited California had established their own religions, culture, and lifestyles, once the Spanish missionaries arrived, they were given little choice in their life. The Spanish Franciscans enforced not only Christianity on the Native Americans, who were known as the neophytes or converts, but also the European colonial way of living. The European missionary movement involved building walled enclosures, where the Native Americans would be forced to live, even if they already had established villages nearby. The converts were taught Spanish along with many traditional European working skills, such as blacksmithing and brickmaking, which they were forced to continue using even after they converted to Christianity, which was done almost always against their will.

Father Junípero Serra's treatment of the native population is of great debate. Although he was, of course, a leading force in the missionary actions in California, he is said to have been less harsh toward the native population than other colonizers. Regardless of how he treated the Native Americans, Mission San Diego was only the first mission of twenty-one set up by Junípero Serra and his successors. The site for Mission San Diego was chosen not only due to its proximity to the port where the explorers' ship docked but also due to its proximity to multiple Native American villages. Father Serra's choice was well placed, as it had easy access to water and was on fertile land, which was necessary, seeing as one element of the missionary conversion process was to enforce European agriculture systems such as traditional vegetable gardens. Over the next thirty years, Mission San Diego would establish extensive European-inspired irrigation systems, which would aid the Native Americans in cultivating tens of thousands of acres.

Around the same time as the establishment of Mission San Diego, Gaspar de Portolá set up the Presidio of San Diego, which was the first permanent European settlement in not only California but also along the Pacific coast. From there, Gaspar de Portolá, Junípero Serra, and various explorers set out on expeditions throughout California in order to set up more missions and presidios (a fortified settlement or military post). In May of 1770, Gaspar de Portolá established the Presidio of Monterey to act as a military base, which the Spaniards felt was necessary due to the Russian threat, which was one of the main reasons Spain suddenly rushed to colonize California. The Russians, who were actively exploring to find the Northwest Passage and hunting otters, seemed as if they were going to make their way down the Pacific coast. The Spanish did not want to encounter the powerhouse without having established some military bases first. Around a month later, Father Junípero Serra established the Mission Monterey, which would later be relocated and become known as the Mission San Carlos Borromeo de Carmelo.

Over the next few years, Gaspar de Portolá and Junípero Serra continued to establish their presence in Alta California, and explorers also reached San Francisco Bay, which is just around 500 miles on land from where San Diego lays. However, colonization did not really take place until after 1773. During the years prior to 1773, Junípero Serra disputed with the Spanish authorities over how Alta California should be run and colonized, and finally, in 1773, he caused the officials to increase financial and military support in California. To begin properly populating the European settlements, the Spanish officials needed to find a safer way to reach the bases in California since the naval route taken by Portolá was not safe for civilians. Though those who had already settled in Alta California had spent some time exploring the area, all of the land passages seemed to be far too hazardous, both because of the unfamiliar and exhausting desert and mountain terrain and because of the threat that could come from crossing through indigenous nations' land. Junípero Serra, who had acquired a great deal of power in California, had been urging the Spanish officials to establish a land route. Regardless of Serra's pleas, Spain knew it needed to find a safe and reliable way to link the various settlements in Mexico and California, as well as those in today's Arizona and New Mexico. With the threat of Russian invasion to the north and rumors of English exploration that could perhaps reach California, Spanish officials felt pressured to immediately begin populating the resource-filled state with both livestock and settlers, which meant they needed to secure a route and fast.

The assignment of finding a safe passage was given to Juan Bautista de Anza, who, having European Spanish ancestors and blood, was born and raised in Mexico and had spent years fighting in various wars as a frontier commander. In January of 1774, Juan Bautista de Anza finally set out on his journey to find a safe passage to California from Tubac, a town located in present-day Arizona, just under twenty-five miles from the Mexican border. Anza led thirty-four men through the dismally hot and dry deserts in present-day Arizona and California and managed to survive due to help from various native nations along the way, namely the Yuma and Cochimí.

Within only a few months, in March, Juan Bautista de Anza and his crew reached Mission San Gabriel, located only ten miles from modern-day Los Angeles. Mission San Gabriel had been established in 1771, making it the fourth mission established in California at the time. Although the group was exhausted after their more than 500-mile trip, the explorers spent the next few months traveling to Monterey, arriving there in May, which added over an extra 300 miles to their journey. Seeing as Juan Bautista de Anza was not just trying to arrive in the Californian settlements but also map out a secure route, it is estimated that the group traveled over 1,000 miles in five months. The group took their own route back to Tubac, perfecting the trail so they could lead civilians and cattle as soon as possible.

Juan Bautista de Anza was approved for a new expedition, and he departed on his next journey around a year later in October of 1775, but this time, he was accompanied by far more than just thirty-four men. Anza led an estimated 240 people who had been living in northern Mexico, including men, women, and children. Alongside the settlers were close to 700 horses and mules and around 350 cattle. After at least three months of travel, the group arrived in San Gabriel, and three months later, in March of 1776, they briefly stopped in Monterey. The large group continued on their journey to develop a new settlement, and by the end of the month, Anza had established the Presidio of San Francisco. Although Anza and his men had spent close to a year searching for the best trail to California, his journey with the 240 civilians would be the final large journey across this path for close to 100 years. After the Yumi revolt in 1781, the Europeans were forced to avoid their territory. A year later, in 1777, Anza's second-in-command, José Joaquín Moraga, led some of the civilians who had set up in

San Francisco to central California and established the Pueblo of San José, which made it the first Spaniard-only town in Alta California.

During this time, Junípero Serra and his associates continued establishing missions. Due to the limited accessibility of California, the Spanish population remained quite small, especially in comparison to the Native American population and the booming American cities on the eastern coast. Despite this, the Native American population was farming enough food to sustain a large city. As part of the missionary process, the neophytes (converts) were taught various agricultural skills, including cattle, grain, olive, wine, and brandy farming and manufacturing. This massive surplus of food allowed the Spanish population to trade with Mexico, allowing the civilians some luxury items, to which early settlements are not usually privy. However, this wealth did not come without a cost, and in this case, it was at the expense of the Native American population. Many thousands of Native Americans were forced to convert to Christianity, and although the native villages often outnumbered the traveling missionaries, the "recruits" were often singled out or followed when alone and then forced to convert, sometimes at gunpoint. To be converted, the Native Americans were baptized, and once baptized, they were essentially bound to the Franciscans' authority. The neophytes worked hard, long hours, adapting to the European agricultural system, which created a surplus of food, but the converts reaped none of the benefits. If a converted Native American disobeyed the Franciscans' authority, it was the law that they could and likely would be whipped or imprisoned. Although the Native American population had established villages and ways of living for thousands of years before the arrival of the Europeans, those who converted were forced into overpopulated walled communities, and they would be hunted down and forced to return or killed if they tried to escape. Due to these horrendous working and living conditions, as well as the many foreign diseases they caught from the Europeans, the once flourishing Native American population in California greatly diminished. Although it is not known exactly how many people had inhabited the state before the arrival of the Europeans, it is estimated that the Native American population diminished by at least 100,000 people within 50 years of Spanish occupation, if not more.

While the Native Americans declined, the population of the European settlers continued to grow and spread out. In 1781, just a few dozen people, including settlers, soldiers, and their families, settled in what was then known as El Pueblo de Nuestra Señora la Reina de los Ángeles (The Town of Our Lady the Queen of the Angels), or the Pueblo of Los Ángeles for short. The city of Los Angeles was officially founded on September 4th, 1781, and though it started small, its population grew steadily. By the 1840s, the population had grown to over 1,000 people, and when California joined the United States of America in 1850, it was the largest settlement in California.

Chapter 4 – Mexican California and The Years before California Joined the United States of America (1821–1846)

In the late 18ᵗʰ century, many colonies claimed independence from their monarchy. The United States is one of the more notable and well-known examples, and it declared independence from British rule in 1776. The same feat began taking place with Spain's many colonies in the early 19ᵗʰ century, starting with Ecuador in 1809, which was soon followed by Bolivia and Peru. The next year, Mexico attempted to declare independence, which began the eleven-year Mexican War of Independence. This war ended with the Treaty of Córdoba in 1821, declaring Mexico to be free from Spanish rule.

Even before Mexico officially gained its independence from Spain, California began feeling the consequences. With Spain being rather distracted in its attempts to protect its rule over its many rebelling colonies, the country could not spare as many resources for the settlements in California as before. California, which had previously only traded with Spanish merchants, mostly those located in Mexico, no longer had access to many of their previous clientele. During the Mexican War of Independence, California had essentially lost all of its trading partners, which led local authorities to ease trading restrictions that had previously limited trade to Spanish merchants. California began trading with various countries, including England, Russia, France, and the nearby United States of America. Although California had felt the changes of other Spanish colonies' rebellions for independence, none would cause as big of a ripple as Mexico's.

The Years following Mexico's Independence from Spain

It took many months for the news that California had been acquired by Mexico when the country gained its independence from Spain to actually reach the Spanish settlers in California. Although California would not technically be designated as a territory of Mexico until 1824, the changes were immense and immediate. Before this, all the settled land in California had been owned and controlled by the Franciscan missionaries, but following 1821, Mexico was determined to change that. Mexico allowed Californians to trade with whomever they liked and encouraged international trade. They also, to the Spanish population's surprise, both allowed and encouraged foreign ownership of land to those who were willing to gain citizenship and convert to Catholicism. This was, of course, an immense change for the Californians, who had only ever known the land to be in the control of the Franciscan authority and, therefore, the Spanish Crown. This was only one of the ways the newly founded Republic of Mexico attempted to secularize the state. Many of the large mission ranches were given to civilians, both of Spanish Californian and of Mexican descent, and with the loss of their land, many of the missionaries withdrew. By 1840, essentially all of the remaining mission lands had been parceled out, and the exploitation of the Native Americans had lessened greatly. That being said, although Mexico enforced the end of violence against the Native American population, they did not receive the majority of the divided mission lands. While they did receive some land, their space was limited and far smaller than it had been before the European occupation.

The majority of those who received land were California-born civilians, who became wealthy, following many years where no one could truly be rich but the government officials sent by the Crown and the church. Although a maximum of around 50,000 acres was legally set aside to ensure the land was split fairly, many individuals, who would begin to form an oligarchy of sorts, would receive multiple land grants. Seeing as these properties were so large and the owners were of the elite class of California, most of these territories, known as California ranchos, would employ Native American workers, made up of both the free and mission native population. Some of these ranchos employed hundreds of Native Americans, and it was estimated that by the mid-19th century, around 4,000 Native Americans were working on these properties. Although the Native Americans were technically free, most became what is known as a serf, which is essentially an agricultural peasant-class laborer forced to work for his or her generally rich lord. The Native Americans received shelter, food, and clothing, but very few were paid money or had any potential for upward momentum. The property lords used various deceitful and violent methods to recruit and then maintain their laborers. Seeing as most Californian manufacturing of products stopped when the missions ended, Californians depended on foreign merchants and traders. Since the merchants were generally seeking hides, the Californian landowners usually pushed most of their laborers to focus on raising cattle.

With the Franciscan authority out of the way, California was instead governed by a Mexican-appointed governor. However, although the new system might have sounded good in theory, the politics in California over the subsequent years were shaky and dramatic. Between the years of 1831 and 1836, California had eleven different governors, as well as three men who almost became governor but were rejected by the Californians. Seeing as the Republic of Mexico had little involvement in the actual territory of California, they had little knowledge of who the Californians would accept as a leader and often named candidates they favored, which caused general dissatisfaction amongst the native-born European Californians. Mexico, which was aware of the potential for rebellions, allowed the Californians to reject whomever they wanted, but they could not appoint or vote for their own leadership. In 1836, the population's discontent culminated in a small revolution in which Juan Bautista Alvarado deported the Mexican officials in Monterey after seizing control of the city. Alvarado preached and demanded that California become its own free and sovereign state. Within a few months, Mexico ceded its appointing power and allowed Alvarado to take the governorship in California, which put an end to the discontent for a while.

Although foreign immigration was allowed, it was mostly uncommon throughout the 1820s. However, over the subsequent decades, immigrants, mostly from the United States, began arriving in California. In 1841, John Bidwell and John Bartleson led a group of a couple of hundred people from Missouri to California. This American immigration was encouraged by various Californian elites and the Western Emigration Society, which feared foreign seizure of California. Upon arriving in California, the group was given shelter at one of the Western Emigration Society's ranchos and jobs working for Johann August Sutter, the German-born Swiss businessman who was known to hire settlers from all over to work on his many orchards, vineyards, and wheat fields. As the American population in California began steadily increasing, the country began growing an interest in procuring California as one of its states.

It was during the Mexican California era that the settlers in California began developing their own unique culture separate from that of Spain's. Bull and bear fights became popular pastimes alongside horse racing. All three activities allowed spectators to place bets on their prospective winner. Although the elite, the common people, and the Native American population all lived in the California territory, it was mostly the elite people who had the privilege to enjoy entertaining pastimes. One luxury that elite families indulged in was abnormally long wedding celebrations, which sometimes lasted for over a week. The bride would change dresses many times through the event, and the united elite families would dance and sing for days.

The Lead-Up to the Mexican-American War

However, despite the entertaining events that were attended joyfully by California's elite, dissatisfaction amongst the Californians was growing, as was the United States' interest in the acquisition of California. Although the Mexican-American War would not begin until 1846, in one of the oddest moments in the history of California, the United States accidentally invaded California prematurely. In 1842, Commodore Thomas ap Catesby Jones, who had been the commanding officer of the US Navy's Pacific Squadron, had heard that the United States and Mexico had begun their war. This was likely a rumor that had materialized due to the United States' growing interest in California, but Jones took this as fact and set sail as he had been instructed to do so. Once the war started, he was supposed to seize Monterey, which was the capital of California at the time. Catching just about everyone off guard, Commodore Jones seized the city of Monterey and raised the United States' star-spangled banner as a sign of victory. However, within the day, Jones learned that his intel was nothing but a rumor, forcing the commodore to apologize to the Republic of Mexico and the Californians. He then returned back to the United States.

Chapter 5 – The Mexican-American War and the United States' Acquisition of California (1846–1848)

Before the start of the Mexican-American War, Californian dissatisfaction toward the Republic of Mexico only grew. In 1842, Mexico sent a governor named Pío de Jesús Pico, often shortened to Pío Pico, from Mexico City. Despite being sent by Mexico, Pío Pico had been born at the Mission San Gabriel in California in 1801 and had had African, Native American, and European descent. His arrival in California was controversial, to say the least, mostly due to the fact that the last governor of California had actually been Juan Bautista Alvarado, who had pioneered a small rebellion against the Republic of Mexico in order to earn the position. Mexico sending one of its appointed governors was, in many ways, a blow to the Californian sense of pride and independence. Within the next year, dissatisfaction continued to rise, and the concept of an American revolution had begun taking shape. At this time, the population of California consisted of around only 100,000 Native Americans, somewhere between 10,000 and 20,000 settlers of both

Spanish or Mexican descent, and less than 3,000 people of foreign descent, of which the largest foreign population was the Americans, whose exact number of inhabitants is unknown.

The Bear Flag Revolt

Although Mexico had instituted many rules upon Americans and other foreigners who attempted to live in California, namely that they had to convert to Catholicism and adopt Mexican citizenship, when Pío Pico took office, he realized enforcing these laws would only lead to a revolution. Pío Pico was essentially left in California by Mexico, which was not helping him or listening to his suggestions or warnings of a potential rebellion. Pico proposed annexing California, which might allow other Western powers to deal with the dissatisfied population instead. However, the government of Mexico would not listen and insisted that they keep California.

Regardless of Mexico's decision not to act in preparation, Pío Pico had been right, and in June of 1846, a small group of Americans living around Sonoma took the city by surprise. They captured the local Mexican colonel, seized the city, and declared independence. To symbolize their freedom, the group raised a handmade flag with a poorly drawn grizzly bear walking toward a red star and the words "California Republic." This is, of course, the origin of the present-day flag of California, which still displays the grizzly bear, red star, and the words "California Republic," although it has gone through many alterations and adjustments over the years. The small group of Americans was led by William B. Ide, who was an American citizen born in Massachusetts, and it slowly moved westward until it finally reached California in late 1845, less than one year before what has come to be known as the Bear Flag Revolt. In the proclamation of the Bear Flag Revolt, William B. Ide called Californians to action by requesting they "assist us in establishing and perpetuating a 'Republican Government' which shall secure to all: civil and religious liberty; which shall detect and punish crime; which shall encourage industry, virtue and literature;

which shall leave unshackled by Fetters, Commerce, Agriculture, and Mechanism." Within the month, Captain John Charles Frémont and his troops arrived in Monterey, prepared to defend their newly acquired city against the Republic of Mexico.

The Mexican-American War

It was at this point that Pío Pico's fears became a reality, and he messaged the Republic of Mexico, urging them to send a defense against the invading American troops. However, once again, Pío Pico's requests went mostly unanswered, and Mexico only sent a few hundred soldiers to attempt to defend California. Aware that the Americans would not appreciate his presence, Pío Pico decided to return to Mexico, but before fleeing, he sold his massive acreage off to various Mexican buyers at low prices.

Despite the fact that Frémont and his troops had seized Sonoma, the era of the Republic of California, as the flag proposed, was short lived, as the Mexican-American War had already begun. Technically, Mexico and the United States had actually been in a war before the American seizure of Sonoma. The war broke out following the annexation of Texas, which, like California, was once the property of Mexico. To make matters worse, after acquiring Texas, the United States began making bids to purchase California and New Mexico, which only angered the Republic of Mexico. The United States had plans to respond to Mexico's refusal to negotiate, but before they had the chance, Mexican troops surprised and attacked American troops patrolling the contested area on April 25th, 1846, injuring and killing many. It was technically this event that kickstarted the Mexican-American War, although it took Captain John Charles Frémont's invasion of California for the war over California to truly begin.

In typical American fashion, the country was rather divided on the prospect of war with Mexico. For the most part, southern Democrats favored the war, while many northern Abolitionists were against the war, as they believed that once America acquired the

Mexican territories in question, they would become slave states. Regardless of the conflicting American opinions, a war with Mexico had begun, and despite many of the elite Californians being against the movement, California had essentially no say. The United States sent troops south to Mexico and west to inhabit California and New Mexico. Although the elite Californian ranchers sided with Mexico, the settlers and Californian civilians showed no resistance to the occupying American soldiers, and many settlers joined the American troops in the fight against the Republic of Mexico. American General Winfield Scott was sent on a campaign through Mexico under the guidance of President James K. Polk. Although Scott's troops were overall extremely successful in battle, seizing city after city on their campaign and only losing around 1,500 soldiers, the United States lost thousands of soldiers to diseases such as yellow fever, measles, mumps, and smallpox. It is estimated that around 10,000 or more American soldiers died from various illnesses on the Mexican front. Poor sanitation and lack of immunity, which was especially common in soldiers from smaller, rural towns, didn't help the matter either. As the war raged on, the Americans easily took California in January of 1847 when John C. Frémont forced the small number of Mexican and elite Californian soldiers to surrender and sign the Capitulation of Cahuenga. Despite the loss of many soldiers due to illness and the strong Mexican resistance, on September 14th, 1847, after many uninterrupted American victories in both Mexico and California, Winfield Scott and his troops seized Mexico City, which put an end to the actual warfare. However, the conflict was far from over.

The End of the Mexican-American War

After seizing Mexico City, President Polk, his chief clerk, Nicholas Trist, and General Winfield Scott met to negotiate a peace treaty that would put an official end to the war. However, the process was continuously delayed. After months of waiting, on February 2nd, 1848, Nicholas Trist impatiently signed the treaty before both parties were ready, and with that move, the Treaty of Guadalupe Hidalgo was finalized. The treaty detailed that the United States would pay Mexico fifteen million dollars in exchange for both the land and the citizens of New Mexico, Utah, Nevada, Arizona, California, Texas, and western Colorado, which, until then, had all been under Mexican control. Although California had now been acquired by the United States, it would not officially become a state until two years later. Many present-day states took years to become an official American state, as one requirement to achieve statehood was a population of 60,000 people. Seeing as California had less than 10,000 people by the end of the Mexican-American War, it was expected to take many years for it to become an official state. However, what was about to happen later in 1848 would skyrocket the population at an unheard-of speed, allowing California to become a state on September 9th, 1850, in only two years' time.

Chapter 6 – The California Gold Rush (1848–1860)

Johann (John) Sutter

Johann August Sutter was a German-born Swiss who had fled fiscal issues in Switzerland for what was, at the time, the Mexican territory of California. Hoping to make something of himself and rid himself of the financial failures he had endured in Switzerland, Sutter persuaded Mexican officials to accord him some fertile land. He was given territory on the Sacramento River by the Mexican governor, which Sutter named New Switzerland (Nueva Helvetia.) Johann August Sutter became known for hiring and offering lavish shelter to American settlers, and most foreign immigrants were told to find Sutter once they arrived in California since he would help them settle. Although Sutter was in debt when he arrived in California, he spent an excessive amount of money on building Sutter's Fort, creating various businesses, and setting up orchards, vineyards, and wheat fields. Johann changed his name to John and emerged as a typical Californian rancho of the time, and although he was kind and welcoming to American laborers, he, much like the other elite landowners, exploited the Native American laborers.

During the Mexican-American War, soldiers arrived to help the US Army in California. The Capitulation of Cahuenga in January of 1847 ended the Californian theater of the Mexican-American War, which means that not only did Mexico surrender but the American soldiers were also stuck waiting until the war ended in the actual Republic of Mexico. Seeing as the war did not end until the Treaty of Guadalupe Hidalgo was signed by Nicholas Trist almost a year later, on February 2nd, 1848, the American soldiers were in need of jobs to bide their time and make some money. John Sutter had become known as the man Americans should go to when they were in need of work, so hundreds arrived at Sutter's Fort in search of odd jobs. Sutter wanted to build a town, which he would name "Sutterville," for some time, and the arrival of all of the soldiers was the perfect opportunity to do so. Sutter decided his first step would be to build a sawmill, which would not only provide employment for the hordes of men arriving on his property but would also create the lumber needed to construct Sutterville. He began searching for a site.

Finding Gold

Sutter hired James Wilson Marshall, a New Jersey-born carpenter, to find the best location for the sawmill, and during 1847, Marshall chose a location around forty-five miles from Sutter's Fort. He was accompanied by various American laborers to build the sawmill and deepen the American River where the mill would be located. The mill was near completion toward the end of 1847, and on January 24th, 1848, Marshall went to check on the sawmill, seeing as the construction was coming to a close. However, when Marshall went down to the river to check on the sawmill, something shining in a ditch caught his eye. In the words of James Marshall, "I reached my hand down and picked it up; it made my heart thump, for I was certain it was gold...Then I saw another." Only nine days before the signing of the Treaty of Guadalupe Hidalgo, which put an end to the Mexican-American War, James Marshall found multiple gold nuggets in the American River, which would drastically change the course of California's history.

The Gold Rush

Seeing as the gold Marshall discovered was on Sutter's property, he quickly relayed the information to his employer, and the two men decided to become partners. Although they tried to keep the fortune a secret, the news leaked. It is hard to know if this was due to the other men who had been working on the sawmill or some other source, but before long, prospective gold miners arrived from all over. Within six months, the hills near the river were covered in tents and wooden huts, which housed over 4,000 men who were prepared to mine for their fortune. The first news of Sutter's fortune reached Asia and then Central and South America. Hundreds of men sailed thousands of miles from China and hiked across Panama, often risking death due to illnesses they'd pick up on the trip as a result of poor sanitation, nutrition, and contact with other populations. While the travelers did suffer, the illnesses killed far more of the Native Americans who came into contact with the prospective gold miners than the gold miners themselves. However, within those first months, the majority of the tents were not of foreigners but of local Californians, which included Hispanic Californians, Sutter's laborers, and Native Americans. Over the course of the next month, some other groups arrived from nearby states and territories such as Utah, Oregon, Hawaii, Mexico, China, and Chile.

The Forty-Niners

Despite news having reached the southern countries in the Americas, it took nearly a year for the news to reach and set in as fact in the United States. Seeing as there was no railroad or easy way to access California as of yet, the news would not reach the eastern United States until boats sailed the Atlantic Ocean on their way for California. Once the news had reached the United States, no one was sure if it was true, and seeing as it was no easy task to reach

California, which by boat would take over half a year, sailing the dangerous waters through the Isthmus of Panama or "around the Horn," citizens were not willing to take a chance on a rumor. By mid-1848, William Tecumseh Sherman, an American army officer, was eager to know if the rumor was true, both for his own curiosity and for his fellow Americans who had no idea of the validity of the rumor. Sherman asked one of his officers, Colonel Richard Barnes Mason, who was California's military governor at the time, if he would go to Sutter's property and see for himself if the rumor was true. Of course, he discovered that there was, in fact, gold to be found. Mason reported the news to President Polk, who proceeded to make an official declaration on December 5th, 1848, sparking a new dream in the American citizens.

That official announcement of gold in California changed California's future in an instant, and by the next day, almost anyone who was left in the territory of California had set up a campsite on the hills near the gold-laden river. However, no one could have expected the insane number of people who arrived over the course of the following year. The immigrants, known as the "forty-niners," arrived in California by the thousands throughout 1849. Tens of thousands of people arrived at San Francisco's port after traveling for miles on the rough oceans, and a few thousand wagons came from all over America, carrying around 40,000 people, despite the hazardous, long, bumpy ride. It is estimated around 80,000 forty-niners arrived over the course of the year, and over 250,000 total had immigrated to California by 1853. They all had one common goal: to hopefully strike gold. Seeing as there was so much competition, only a lucky few actually struck gold, and since the locals knew they could take advantage of the newcomers, the cost of living and food was high. Those who were tired of digging or had some starter money opened businesses, stores, and/or became farmers, which helped develop California's local economy. Before the Gold Rush, its economy was practically non-existent. Despite the hard, strenuous work and long hours, the gold miners rarely got a full night's sleep, seeing as they lived in overpopulated areas and typically slept in primitive shelters, such as tents and huts. However, seeing as two billion dollars in gold was extracted from the river and surrounding areas, many did strike gold, and they would generally invest in hiring miners to continue looking for them until they could replace the laborers with machines.

California Becoming a State

Although there are many different requirements set in place for a territory to become an official state in the United States of America, in 1848, when America officially acquired California, the main thing in California's way was the population requirement. At the time, California needed to have 60,000 people for it to officially achieve statehood, and when it was won by the United States as a result of the Mexican-American War, California only had a measly 7,000 people or so. Many states took years until they had a large enough population to gain statehood, and since California's population was so small, it seemed like it could take at least a decade for enough Americans to emigrate to California. However, all of that changed with Sutter and Marshall's discovery of gold in January of 1848 in present-day Sacramento. In 1849, far more than 60,000 people arrived, meaning that California blew past the required population number to join the Union and become an official state. Although there were many debates, on September 9th, 1850, California was officially recognized as a state by Congress. This decision was sped up not only by the discovery of gold but also by the fact that rancheros and local commanders were impatiently waiting on reforms that could best be decided by a central government. They decided to draw up their own constitution modeled after those of other states. The constitution declared California as a free-labor state, meaning that it was anti-slavery and that laborers were independent of their employers and could technically work their way to riches. As an interesting side note, California was never a designated territory of the United States, unlike other states out west, such as Oregon.

After 1850

In the years prior to California achieving statehood, laws were created and upheld by local miners and townspeople, who, without any official government, were forced to handle local affairs themselves. However, even after September 9th, 1850, when California joined the United States, no central government truly took control of the state, and local officers did not want to act without instruction, which frustrated the local civilians. By 1851, the dissatisfied people in San Francisco formed a law-and-order group called the "Vigilance Committee," which inspired other mining towns and Californian cities to do the same. Although this worked for a short period, by the end of the year, most of the groups had disbanded, and local authorities took control.

By the end of the Gold Rush, more than 300,000 people had permanently emigrated to California. In many of the Gold Rush towns, there were businesses and economies set up around the mines, but in others, there was nothing but a ghost town, as once the gold supply had dried up, the miners would pack up and leave. In the years following 1852, the Gold Rush slowed down, especially as technologies improved. Beforehand, the panning method was the most common way to find gold. This method involved an individual miner swirling water in a strainer. However, with time came the wooden "rocker" and other creations that changed the face of mining. The majority of these mining inventions were more efficient, as they allowed many laborers to work together rather than just one individual man working on his own. As a result, the richer miners formed companies. Soon enough, the gold in the rivers was all excavated, and the miners moved to the nearby rocks, where they mined shafts with pickaxes dozens of feet in the ground. Underground tunnels began stretching across many miles, and men working in teams for large businesses spent their days below ground, searching for gold. Although many of the miners who had hoped to strike it rich on their own had left after the 1850s, over the next few decades, the gold hunt still existed, and it was dominated by large joint-stock companies rather than individual men.

The Effects of the Gold Rush

It is without a doubt that the effects of the Gold Rush dramatically changed the territory of California. Although not many individuals became rich from the rush itself, plenty of businessmen and shop owners profited greatly off of the booming population and the need for entertainment, food, shelter, and other resources. Settlers from all over the globe arrived in California, which had previously only been made up of Native Americans, Spanish Californians, and Mexicans. The Gold Rush caused the population to grow almost twenty times as large in less than a decade, and it is the reason California was admitted as a state so quickly. With the new influx of people, California was forced to build up its cities, and a local economy developed. California would quickly become the biggest powerhouse in western America, both economically and politically. Immigrants benefited from California's vast expanse of available land, many fishable waterways, ideal farming climate, and fertile soil.

Chapter 7 – California during the Civil War and in the First Few Years of Development (1860–1869)

Initial Societal Issues

By the beginning of the 1860s, the population of California had well surpassed 300,000 residents, and seeing as the census did not usually take into account the many spread-out native tribes around the state, there was likely more than 300,000. Since the start of the Gold Rush, the population had tripled, but by 1860, gold mining was no longer the main resource attracting immigrants. California had mild temperatures, exceptionally long growing seasons, and fertile soil. All types of farming flourished over the decades following the Gold Rush, but cattle ranching was likely the most profitable in the 1860s. The farmers and manufacturers who arrived alongside the gold miners were much needed in the newly founded state, which had been relying on foreign merchants for most manufactured items since the expulsion of the Franciscan missionaries by the Republic of Mexico. However, despite the fact that California's internal production was increasing and its own local market was growing, farmers, manufacturers, producers, and businessmen were all very aware of the losses they experienced due to the lack of a link to the rest of the United States. Unlike many of the cities elsewhere in the United States, which had boomed gradually as railways were built and cities expanded, the California Gold Rush pushed California's population to grow far faster than cities usually do, which meant the state's cities were not quite prepared for the needs of a large permanent society.

The lack of a railway was not the only way California's cities were not prepared for large permanent settlements. Toward the mid-19th century, many issues arose between different ethnic groups who had arrived in California for the same purpose, to make a fortune or at least some money for themselves and their family. Although American citizens who had arrived from the eastern states generally seemed to get along with European immigrants, whether they spoke the English tongue or not, they generally resented non-English-speaking and non-European miners and civilians. Prejudice and racial issues began arising between the American miners and the Latin and Chinese miners. Over time, the mining population migrated away from the Gold Rush rivers and mines and to the newly established cities. Many of the Chinese miners congregated in San Francisco, where they settled and opened businesses, establishing the United States of America's very first Chinatown. The Chinese who continued to search for gold continued to feel harsh treatment from their American peers, who had developed a racist anti-Chinese mindset. This meant that California not only became a difficult place for the diverse foreigners who had arrived throughout the 19th century but also for the Americans, especially those from the Confederate States, who were not used to foreigners and had little respect or understanding of the diversity of California.

California's Relationship with Slavery

Another massive societal issue the newly founded Californian cities were forced to deal with was the varying opinion on slavery. Although the Californian constitution had technically ordained California as a free-labor state, the agreement was not exactly specific, and there were many easy ways to find loopholes in the text. It was not only the Californians who were unsure about their stance on slavery but also the other states, which often fought about how strict California's slavery stance should be. This debate is part of the reason why California was not admitted as a state in 1849, even though it had met the population requirement. During the Gold Rush, businessmen and mining companies from the Confederate States sent hundreds if not thousands of African slaves to mine for gold. Though California was determined as a free-labor, anti-slave state, one way these slave owners got around the rules was by not officially declaring the slaves as citizens. Instead, they were workers and were designated as citizens for states that allowed slavery. Thus, while slavery was occurring on Californian soil, the rules were vague enough that there were rarely consequences. By 1860, there were a few thousand African Americans living in California, the majority of them living freely in San Francisco, Sacramento, and other smaller mining towns in the north, where slavery was commonly rejected and the population was less prejudiced.

Overall, the issue of slavery was not settled in California as it may have seemed to have been when the country formed its constitution. The state was essentially separated into those known as Free Soilers in the north, who believed California should be a free state, and those who were self-titled the Chivs (shortened from chivalry) in the south, who wanted California to be a slave state. This split was no different than what many of the southern states had been seeing. Something similar occurred in the state of Virginia, which ended up splitting into the anti-slavery state of West Virginia and pro-slavery

Virginia. Although the state of California was never technically separated, nor was it the common opinion that separation should occur, the difference of opinions toward slavery only caused more societal issues for the newly forming cities and growing population in California.

California's Role in the Civil War

Although the state of California had been and is still to this day overwhelmingly Democratic-leaning, at the time of the 1860 presidential election, Republican candidate Abraham Lincoln won the majority in California, albeit only by a small margin. There are a number of reasons as to why California suddenly voted Republican, one being that the businessmen who held a lot of power and property in California were mostly Republican. The other reason is likely that the state was not, for the most part, pro-slavery, which was a key part of the Democratic Party's campaign. However, despite the fact that Lincoln won in California, the votes were closer than in almost any other state, as the other states generally had a sweeping majority vote during the 1860 presidential election. The differences of opinion on slavery were, of course, not only an issue in California, and by 1861, just after Lincoln's inauguration, the American Civil War broke out between the Union (anti-slavery) and the Confederate (pro-slavery) states. Despite the fact that there were still many powerful Californian southerners who believed slavery was their right, during the Civil War, California supported the anti-slavery Union armies. This led some of the dissatisfied Californian southerners to create pro-Confederate groups, such as the well-known Los Angeles Mounted Rifles and the Knights of the Golden Circle.

California would be a great help to the Union military by providing both soldiers and financing. Although California was far away from most of the fighting, many believe that it was, in fact, California's gold mines that helped sway the course of the war in favor of the Union. The state of California was rather remote when the Civil War broke out, but the state still supplied the Union military with thousands of soldiers. They mainly helped fight in nearby states, such as Arizona and New Mexico. After the initial attack on Fort Sumter, which is what began the Civil War, many anti-slavery Californians were inspired to join the military, and by the end of the war, over 17,000 Californians enlisted. Despite the state's distance from most of the fighting, California would actually have the highest Union military joining per capita ratio in all of America, which was partly because the population of California was still quite small at the start of the Civil War. Those who could not join the military also held pro-Union rallies, most notably in San Francisco, which would help inspire many men to join the movement over the course of the war.

Despite the large number of Californian soldiers who ended up supporting the Union military, California's largest contribution to the war was not in manpower but in financial and material contributions. California was one of the largest funders of the United States Sanitary Commission, a Union medical organization. To help fund the Union organizations, military, and government, California sent shipments of gold out to the Union forces in any way possible. Seeing as there were still no railways at the time of the outbreak of the American Civil War, the safest way to get gold to the Union was by ship, which mostly sailed from the San Francisco Bay. The United States government began sending Union military troops to San Francisco in order to protect the gold shipments, which sometimes amounted to over a million dollars. Typically, lesser amounts would be shipped out, but all these shipments were constantly threatened by Confederate raiders on steamships.

Building the Railway

After many years of isolation, the necessity for a railroad connecting the rest of the United States of American to California increased. It seemed as if the construction of a railway could no longer wait, and in 1862, Abraham Lincoln signed the Pacific

Railway Act. Although California had become an official state in 1850, construction had been delayed due to many debates over whether the railways should be built through the North or the South of the United States. Of course, when President Lincoln signed the Pacific Railway Act in 1862, the decision was made that the railway would be built in the North, with the intention of helping the Union forces in the American Civil War and avoiding enemy forces who may raid the Union trains if it was built in the South.

Although the debate had ended as to where the railway would be built, the task of completing the railway would be far from easy. Between California and the eastern United States stood hundreds of miles of grueling deserts, high mountain elevations, and waterways that would have to be crossed. Seeing as the tracks would not be laid with modern technological machines, such as bulldozers or even explosives, the work would be exhausting, dangerous, and extensive.

The work began in 1863, but since few Americans wanted or were even capable of working on the Pacific railroad, the Central Pacific Railroad company depended on Chinese laborers. Although there was quite a lot of prejudice against the Chinese at the time, the railway agreed to hire some of the Chinese workers who had been inhabiting California at the time, mostly with the intention of motivating the European and American men, who felt they could lounge and argue over wages since essentially nobody wanted their jobs. The Chinese laborers not only impressed the project heads but also blew the American and European workers out of the water, as they proved to be far more punctual, efficient, and physically capable of withstanding the grueling conditions. The Central Pacific Railroad began hiring thousands of Chinese laborers, with the main advantage being they could pay them far less. Despite the fact that the Union Army was actively fighting against the use of slavery, the Chinese men who worked to build the Central Pacific Railroad were mistreated and poorly paid. While they were not technically slaves, they endured hazardous, life-threatening work with almost no pay or reward of any kind.

The transcontinental railway was built from both directions with the plan to meet in the middle, and on May 10th, 1869, after six years of gruesome labor done mostly by the Chinese workers, the Central Pacific and Union Pacific Railroads were connected. For the first time in history, Californians had access to the rest of America without the need for many months of sailing or hazardous hikes across the deserts and mountains.

Chapter 8 – California Post Civil War until the End of the 19th Century (1865–1900)

The Expansion of the Railroads and the Impact on California's Cities

Although there had already been some short local railroads built in and around California during the Gold Rush, there were no railroads connecting the state to far-off destinations, but the lack of railroads didn't stop people from arriving during the 1840s and 1850s. However, the transcontinental railroad, which was built by the Central Pacific and Union Pacific Railroads and completed on May 10th, 1869, would drastically change California's immigration patterns. The western terminus had been constructed in Sacramento, although the ultimate goal was to have the transcontinental railway reach the booming city of San Francisco. Originally, train passengers would get off the train in Sacramento and then embark on paddle steamers that would take them to nearby cities, including San Francisco. However, on September 6th, 1869, the Western Pacific Railroad completed the railway that would connect Sacramento and the San Francisco Bay so that routes could end at the Alameda Terminal, only ten miles or so by boat to San Francisco. A few months later, the terminus was moved a few miles north to Oakland, which would facilitate the connection of the transcontinental line to the rest of California's cities. Initially, the arrival of the transcontinental railroad had the effect California had expected: the northern cities that the train line reached expanded their economies and population as drastically as during the Gold Rush. However, what the northern businessmen, who had pushed for the railway, had not expected was the expansion in the south of California over the next few decades, which would take power and business away from the previously booming north.

When the transcontinental railroad reached the north of California, passengers moving to settle and farm would quickly discover that almost all of the area within one hundred miles or more of the terminus was already owned by big businesses, which were hoping to capitalize off the passengers, and by large ranchos that had been kept in the family since the time of Mexico's ownership of California. Although many easterners settled in the ever-expanding city of San Francisco, those looking to farm and own some property quickly began to spread southward in search of vacant land. By the 1880s, the state of California had lowered the ticket costs to promote travel and expanded the railroad hundreds of miles southward. In 1885, the railroad finally reached Los Angeles, which had a population of just over 10,000 people at the time. Within the next decade, the population of Los Angeles and Southern California grew by tens of thousands, and by the turn of the century, there would be over 100,000 people in Los Angeles alone.

As the railroads expanded, companies bought up all of the land surrounding the terminuses with the intention of constructing buildings that suited every type of buyer and traveler who was arriving. Throughout the end of the 19th century, California became littered with resort hotels, official state parks, and other gimmicks to bring in tourists who would hopefully settle and help grow California's economy.

California's Tourism Scene

Just about every American, even those with no intention of settling in California, were interested in visiting the state. Between their fascination with the Gold Rush and the promotions from the railroads and businessmen of California advertising unique landscapes of the state, California quickly became a popular tourist spot and a dream destination for many eastern Americans. In 1865, even Abraham Lincoln was quoted to have said, "I have long desired to see California; the production of her gold mines has been a marvel to me...I have it now in purpose when the railroad is finished, to visit your wonderful state." Although many of the temporary travelers arriving on the trains to California had the intention of striking it rich mining for gold, which by the time of the train lines had become something of a fool's errand, others arrived just to see the Gold Rush in action after hearing rumors of the frenzy for years. As the train line expanded, the gold mines were no longer the only destinations advertised to travelers. Tourists began seeking out California's unique landscape, the Pacific coastline, redwood forests, and the cliffs and waterfalls of the Yosemite Valley. The railroads and big California companies and businesses quickly realized it was becoming more profitable to set up businesses near attractions for tourists than for Californian locals, so hotels, themed restaurants, and pre-packaged tours became more and more common.

California's Conservationism Movements

As big businesses and the railroad companies began profiting off of California's tourism by setting up hotels, railways, and stores, more and more of California's land was being eaten up by tourist attractions. Although many tourists were happy to get on the train, stay in the gimmicky hotels, go on some tours of California's unique landscapes, and then head back home, other tourists were noticing how the landscapes were actually being transformed and destroyed by the tourism. It was California's jaw-dropping glacial Yosemite Valley that inspired Scottish-born John Muir to find a way to protect the state's incredible flora and fauna. John Muir arrived in California just after the transcontinental train line was completed, and after spending some years working and traveling in California, he noticed how the state that he had fallen in love with was changing around him. Muir began connecting with other nature lovers in the Sierra Club, and together, the group founded a conservation movement whose main goal was to protect the natural wonders of California. The conservation group, as well as others inspired by Muir and his fellow Californian nature lovers, began getting in contact with the state and national governments in order to put some rules in place that would preserve as much nature as possible. Although the group would have many small successes during the 1870s and 1880s, in 1890, they achieved Muir's original goal of protecting the Yosemite Valley with the creation of Yosemite National Park.

California's Native American Population during the Late 19th Century

John Muir and the other conservationists were not the only ones attempting to protect California's nature and landscape against the big businesses and railroad ventures. While the boom in population benefited many of the American Californians who had set up businesses during the Gold Rush, it caused mass destruction to the population who had been living there previously. The Native Americans of California had suffered with every new immigration pattern that had arrived in the state, with the expansion of the railroads perhaps one of the worst things to happen to the native population to date. As the Americans arrived in hordes on the trains, planning to settle in the lands in the south and east that had not been bought and developed by businesses, the Native American territory continued to get smaller and smaller. History repeated itself when the native population, which had reestablished their migratory ways of living over the previous decades, were forced into communities on small restricted preserved lands known as reservations, similar to when California was under Franciscan authority. The native tribes, which had just found freedom from the ranchos and managed to find space during the Gold Rush to live their migratory lifestyles away from the coast where the Americans had settled, were once again being shoved out of their own territories. With every given year, the railroads expanded their tracks, bringing along Americans and Europeans who gradually settled on more and more of the previously occupied native land. As more settlers arrived, the Native American reservation lands became more and more unfavorable, as the fertile territories were given to prospective white American farmers. The Native Americans were forced to get used to the pattern. The railroads expanded, they were moved to a smaller territory, settlers found something of interest while exploring nearby territories, and the native tribes were once again moved, their territory gradually being reduced and migration becoming no longer possible.

Of course, the Native American population was not just amicably allowing the settlers to take their land, and many tribes, which were small to begin with, were almost completely wiped out trying to stick up for their land. Even the Native American success stories were rarely positive, seeing as victories only lasted until the next settlers arrived. One of the most well-known examples of the far from harmonious Native American and white American relations was in the Modoc War, which lasted from 1872 to 1873. Before the 1860s, the Modoc population lived peacefully in the Tule Lake region in northeast California. However, in 1864, after many years of living remotely, virtually in isolation, Americans who had arrived for the Gold Rush wanted to settle and mine in the Modoc tribe's territory. The United States created a reservation for them to move to in Klamath, Oregon, around forty miles away from their previous territory in Tule Lake, California. Aware of the potential for war and knowing that the Americans would be more prepared than them, the Modoc population moved as peacefully as possible to the granted reservation land in southern Oregon. Although the Modoc population resentfully resituated themselves in their new territory, they planned to find a way to return to their home. Finally, in 1870, around 175 of the Modoc who had been moved to the Klamath reservation returned to Tule Lake under the leadership of Kientpoos (known as Captain Jack). The group remained there for almost two years until US Army commanders were instructed to, if possible, peacefully return the Modoc to their reservation. Of course, the angered Native Americans were not willing to peacefully return to the government reservation, and by 1873, the US Army's orders changed, and they were instructed to use more force to remove the Modoc people from their homeland. Thus began the Modoc War.

On January 17th, 1873, 400 armed men from the United States Army, most of whom were on horseback, surprised and attacked the 50 or so Modoc who were defending Tule Lake. Although the Modoc population was caught off guard, they knew the unique landscape of lava beds and cliffs well, and they used it to their advantage. Despite the fact that the Americans had advanced Civil War weaponry in comparison to the Native Americans' slow, out-of-date muzzle-loading weapons, the Modoc managed to kill a few dozen American soldiers and forced the rest to retreat. Following that brief violent interaction, the Modoc's leader Kientpoos (Captain Jack), accompanied by other Modoc, met with General Edward Canby to discuss peaceful solutions. The period of peace and discussion lasted a few months, but within time, the Modoc stopped arriving at scheduled meetings, and both sides became aggravated. On April 11th, 1873, the two sides had planned to have a peaceful discussion, but both the US soldiers and the Modoc people showed up armed. At the April 11th meeting, Kientpoos (Captain Jack), who was determined to find a solution, requested a promise from General Canby that the Modoc tribe could have a place in their homeland, which Canby could not promise. This was the straw that broke the camel's back, and the Modoc tribe attacked and killed General Canby. Canby was the only US Army general to die in the overarching American Indian Wars, so it is safe to say that after his death on April 11th, the United States Army was beyond peaceful agreements. On April 15th, the United States Army sent 600 soldiers to attack the Modoc, and after only a few days of fighting, they forced the Modoc people to split up and flee eastward. Of course, the United States soldiers were not going to allow the Modoc tribe to get away after killing their general, and over the course of the next month, the Modoc groups were pursued. Within time, one of the small Modoc groups that had split off from the main assembly was captured, and it agreed to help the United States Army track down the rest of the Modoc and, more specifically, their leader Kientpoos (Captain Jack). The rest of the Modoc were captured on June 1st, and while most were sent to various Oklahoma reservations, four months later, Captain Jack and six other Modoc were hung on account of murder. It would be thirty-six years before the Modoc that had been sent to the reservations in Oklahoma were allowed to return to their families on the Klamath reservations. The Modoc people lost their homeland, and by losing their home, they also lost their lifestyle, diet, artistry, traditions, and other ways of life that were unique to their location. Although the Modoc tribe put up a good fight, they had little chance against the United States Army, which had not only far more people and more advanced weapons but also money. In just the Modoc War alone, the United States Army spent 500,000 dollars.

The Modoc were far from the only tribe to be pushed out of their ancestral home by the settlers and United States Army. Throughout what is known as the American Indian Wars, hundreds of tribes were forced onto reservations, and thousands of Native Americans lost their life. While this was occurring all over the United States, the previously diverse and peaceful Californian tribes were hit especially hard, and by 1900, there was only estimated to be about 15,000 Native American people left in California. Although the main reason for the Native American population decreasing from over a hundred thousand to only 15,000 was displacements to other states, thousands of Native Americans died due to war or illnesses brought by tourists and settlers.

Mexican Californians and California Ranchos during the Late 19th Century

Although not as destructive as it was to the Native American population, the arrival of the new American settlers over the course of the 19th century was not entirely positive for the other Californians who had thrived in the territory before the Gold Rush. While the elite Mexicans in California still did quite well during the 1850s, many white American miners developed prejudices toward Mexican and Hispanic miners during the Gold Rush. Over the years, this prejudice reached even the richest of California's Mexicans. As American settlers arrived, hoping to purchase land in California, many were disappointed to find out that much of the land along the Pacific coast and near the expanding cities had been granted to Mexican and Spanish civilians after the expulsion of the Franciscan missionaries. Discussion of whether these land grants should still be valid, seeing as the territory had not been bought and now belonged to the United States, became commonplace. Mexican and Spanish landowners were forced to spend thousands of dollars in court disputing their case, which, even if they won, often drained them of the money needed to upkeep the property. Over the course of the decades following the Gold Rush, the white American population began gradually outnumbering the Mexican population, and within time, the Mexicans and Hispanics lost most of their power in the state of California. By the 1880s, the Spanish and Mexican population would become a small minority of the population, and they would be mostly forgotten by the growing white American population. It would not be until the 20th century, when Spanish and Mexican immigration recommenced, that the

---

Spanish and Mexican population began to be able to have more of a say in California's politics and lifestyle once again.

Feminism in California

Although equality of the genders was nowhere near present-day standards, overall, California was more progressive than other American states in the mid-19th century. Of course, women were still not able to vote, and the "progressive" rights were only accorded to white women in California. However, white wives were technically able to own property in 1850, which was not common in southern states. Although California would not allow women to vote until 1911, in 1884, a Californian feminist politician, Marietta L. Stow, became the first female to run for vice president of the United States. While Marietta L. Stow was faced with inequality herself, her tagline while running for the governor of California was "anti-monopoly, anti-ring, and anti-Chinese." This was common, as the various groups of minorities (and those who faced inequality) in California were no less prejudiced against each other than the white Americans.

Chinese Population in California toward the End of the 19th Century

If Marietta L. Stow's political 1880s campaign, "anti-monopoly, anti-ring, and anti-Chinese," was of any indication, throughout the 19th century, the prejudice against the Chinese immigrants only worsened. During the Gold Rush, tens of thousands of Chinese immigrants arrived alongside foreigners from the United States, Europe, and South America, and discrimination against the Chinese in the mining camps began almost immediately. By the 1860s and 1870s, as gold mining transitioned into being owned by big corporations instead of individual miners, the majority of the Chinese immigrants who had arrived for the Gold Rush had moved to rural areas. Although most of California's population by the turn of the century had arrived on train tracks laid by Chinese immigrants who had been living in California during the Gold Rush, when the national economy worsened in the 1870s, many Americans felt that it was unfair for the Chinese laborers to be hired while there were "Americans" without work. Technically, it was true that Chinese laborers had been given many jobs, jobs that may have gone to "Americans," but this was mainly due to the fact that there were no regulations against paying the minorities less than white Americans working the same job. The Chinese were being taken advantage of by bosses who would not have hired white Americans to work the job in the first place since it would cost them more. The reputation of the Chinese was not helped by the fact that Chinese immigrants continued to arrive over the course of the 1870s, which made Americans discriminate more against Chinese Americans, some of who had lived in California for two decades or more, as they felt their work was even more threatened than before. In 1880, the United States would begin to regulate Chinese immigration, and in 1882, the United States signed the Chinese Exclusion Act, which put an end to Chinese immigration altogether until 1890.

Although the majority of the Chinese immigrants who arrived to mine gold in the 1850s immediately went to work on farms in rural areas after the Gold Rush came to an end, 24 percent of the Chinese population in California moved to San Francisco. San Francisco had become a safe place or at least the safest place for Chinese immigrants in the state of California. As the city's Chinatown grew, Chinese Americans could expect to find restaurants with the food they grew up with, work under people who spoke their language, and fellow Chinese speakers to become friends with. As anti-Chinese sentiment grew and was openly displayed in rallies and protests, the Chinese population was thriving in San Francisco (at least in comparison to other states and areas in California), and before long, many of the Chinese immigrants who had been working in the rural areas moved to the cities. By the turn of the century, more than half of California's Chinese population had moved to urban areas, 45 percent of which were actually living in and around San Francisco.

The majority of the Chinese immigrants in California were men since most immigrants had the intention of striking it rich during the California Gold Rush and returning home to their families or bringing their families to California. The Chinese women in California had it quite a bit worse than the men. The workforce for women in California was already limited, and on top of the anti-Chinese prejudice, women had an almost impossible time finding work. Those who managed to make it to California were often tricked into becoming essentially slaves of the sex trade, and in 1870, over 60 percent of Chinese women in California were prostitutes, with no way to get out of the unfair contracts.

California Heading into the New Century

If California's history in the mid-19th century is defined by the Gold Rush and its many effects, California between the end of the Civil War until the turn of the century can almost entirely be defined by the completion of the railway. Regardless of the often-disastrous effects on the Chinese, Mexican, Spanish, and Native American populations, California was expanding at record rates. By the 1890s, California had already had its first real estate boom and real estate collapse; tourism was being established, with buildings to accommodate tourists being built so quickly that conservatism was founded; and the Native American population had been reduced to merely 5 percent of what it had been before the Gold Rush. With almost all of the state's gold being excavated, California began developing its own unique diversified economy with mining of other minerals, as well as farming that had not yet been accessible to America. However, by 1900, California was no longer the only state in the West, as the entire Pacific coast had been established by newly formed American states. Overall, despite the inequality amongst the races, over the course of the 19th century and still in the present day, California became a desirable location for most immigrants coming to the United States hoping to achieve the "American Dream."

Chapter 9 – California in the 20th Century (1900–2000)

Unlike most states and cities, which received more organized immigration and gradual economic growth, California's Gold Rush created a population boom that the state was not yet prepared for. The cities were small and unfit for the influx of people, and the local economy was unestablished, but by the beginning of the 20th century, the peak of the Gold Rush had ended over half a century ago. In 1850, the population of California was 92,597, and by 1900, the population had grown to 1,485,053 people, many of whom had arrived far after the Gold Rush had ended. By the turn of the century, the over a million people who now inhabited California had established ways to build the local Californian economy, with one of the primary ways being oil production. In 1855, oil was discovered less than forty miles away from the still small Los Angeles in Pico Canyon, and in 1865, another oil well was unearthed in Humboldt County of Northern California. When the oil was discovered, America did not have much of a need for it, but over the course of the 19th and 20th centuries, the demand for oil would skyrocket, as automobiles became commonplace. By the year 1900, California was one of the leading oil-producing states in the United States, which would help establish California's economy and workforce and give immigrants another reason to choose California to settle in.

San Francisco Earthquake

Despite the fact that California's economy and the population were growing at record speeds with every passing year, the cities were oftentimes ill-equipped for the incoming settlers, and, in turn, the settlers were ill-equipped for California's unique topography, climate, and natural occurrences. No different than the present day, the state of California was no stranger to forest fires, floods, and earthquakes, and while all of which could be destructive, the Native American communities who had lived in the territory before had adopted strategies to cope with the potential natural disasters. The American settlers, on the other hand, were, for the most part, used to eastern climates and nature, which, in comparison to California, is much more stable. They were not prepared for the potential natural disasters. As buildings went up, few had been constructed with natural disasters in mind, which is why the San Francisco earthquake of 1906 hit California so hard.

Although San Francisco and the state of California had experienced other earthquakes, namely two only a few years beforehand in 1898 and 1900, on the morning of April 18th, 1906, San Francisco and the state of California was hit with an earthquake the likes the settlers had never experienced before. Before sunrise, the city of San Francisco was hit with a 7.7 to 7.9 magnitude earthquake, which was described to have sounded "like the roar of 10,000 lions." At five in the morning, the entire city shook, and seeing as the city was not prepared, glass roofs shattered all over the streets, City Hall crumbled, and many massive uncontrollable fires spread around the city. Although the earthquake of 1906 was beyond damaging, it would be the fire that caused the most destruction in the city. The fire, which raged on for three more days, destroyed close to 30,000 buildings on around 500 blocks in the, at this point, newly constructed San Francisco. Seeing as firemen of the early 20th century were still ill-equipped for fighting fires and those in California were almost completely inexperienced in fighting massive fires, the fire department was unable to put out the fire, and it would not be until the rain fell on April 21st that the fire would be put out once and for all. In less than a week, the city was destroyed; it is estimated around 350 million dollars' worth of property was lost and that around 4,000 people died due to the earthquake and resulting fires.

The earthquake, which lasted for only a minute, would cause effects that would ripple throughout the entire state of California. Due to San Francisco's response to the event, it became quickly obvious how common class, race, and political issues were in the state of California. Following the 1906 earthquake and fires, a quarter of a million people were left homeless, driving a wedge even further between the elite upper-class citizens and the working class who had suffered the greatest. Seeing as the city of San Francisco needed to be rebuilt, relief money quickly came flooding in from the United States, whose president at the time was Theodore Roosevelt, as well as from European and Asian countries that had become well-acquainted trade partners with the state of California. The rebuilding of the city was put into the hands of the mayor, James Phelan, and his formed committee of the city's rich businessmen, who quickly set up cramped, poorly taken care of refugee camps for San Francisco's homeless.

Although inequalities between the working class and the elite have technically existed in California since the very beginning of its history, it became more obvious by how the committee responded to the 1906 crises in San Francisco. Although 250,000 people had lost their homes to the fires and earthquake, rather than focusing on rebuilding homes, the committee set up refugee camps and focused on rebuilding businesses. Those who had been poor before 1906 suffered the worst since the poorer communities often lived and worked in the same buildings, which meant that if someone lost their workplace to the fire or earthquake, they lost their home as well. The various racial minorities in San Francisco, who already had it hard enough, suffered greatly from the events of 1906. Almost all of San Francisco's Chinatown burnt down in the fires, which many directly associate to the committee's attempts to protect the Nob Hill neighborhood, where many of the wealthy city leaders resided, as they used dynamite on Chinatown buildings to slow down the spread of the fire. However, this action not only destroyed Chinese homes and businesses but also fueled the flames. After the rain put out the fire, soldiers, who were instructed to protect and guard the city, turned a blind eye and allowed men, women, and fellow soldiers to loot Chinatown of anything that had survived the fire, meaning the Chinese lost everything they owned of value, even what didn't burn. Lootings became commonplace occurrences in the aftermath of the earthquake and fires, and the ill-equipped police force was instructed to shoot looters. However, they would often disproportionately shoot racial minorities, although almost all of the poor civilians were looting at the time. San Francisco was gradually rebuilt with fires, earthquakes, and other natural disasters in mind to avoid any other crises such as what occurred in 1906, and as the other cities in California were built, city planners learned from San Francisco and planned ahead.

Expansion of the South of California

Following the events of the San Francisco earthquake and fires of 1906, San Francisco and, by proxy, Northern California became less desirable for new settlers. Although California's population would increase by 60 percent by 1910, the majority of the population was no longer heading for the San Francisco Bay Area but the ever-expanding south of California. In 1900, San Francisco represented almost a quarter of California's population, with around 342,782 people living there, but by 1910, the population had grown by less than 100,000 people even though California's overall population had grown by close to a million.

The south of California, which was now easily accessible from the train lines, was rumored to have incredible growing conditions, and it was growing at record speeds, with most of the growth centered specifically around Los Angeles, which had the advantage of nearby oil wells. At the turn of the century, Los Angeles's population was just barely over 100,000, but within a decade, the population had grown to 319,198, and by 1920, the population of Los Angeles would have tens of thousands of more people than San Francisco. Part of this rise in population was due to the influx of Mexican immigrants who arrived over the course of the 1910s as the country dealt with its bloody years of revolution. The other reason for the growth in population was the creation of the film industry, which boomed at the beginning of the 20th century, bringing hordes of prospective movie stars to Hollywood. They were no different than the forty-niners of Gold Rush, as they too had dreams of becoming rich.

The Film Industry

In many foreigners' eyes, California is now synonymous with Hollywood and its film industry. Hollywood's first film, *The Count of Monte Cristo*, was completed in 1908, but Hollywood's film industry would not truly begin to pick up steam until the 1910s. Until the 20th century, all American films had been produced on the East Coast, but in 1908, when Thomas Edison founded the Motion Picture Patents Company, which essentially wiped out the United States' film industry companies with costly lawsuits, the film companies began moving as far away from Edison as possible. In 1910, the first film was shot entirely in California, and by 1911, California's first movie studio opened on Hollywood's Sunset Boulevard. California became the perfect location for filmmakers. It had predictable weather, optimal sunlight, every type of background landscape, and, best of all, the filmmakers could not be sued by the Motion Picture Patents Company. As movie production increased in California, featuring beautiful idyllic shots of nature, the state essentially received free advertising, and hordes of settlers arrived, both to be in the movies and to visit the settings the movies depicted.

World War I

Although California and the other western states were far less involved in World War I, as well as other wars, than the eastern American states, the state of California still played its part during the Great War, which lasted from 1914 to 1918. Throughout World War I, California's greatest contribution was to the Allies' aviation sector of the military. During World War I, nearly 200,000 employees worked in the aircraft industry in California, and by the end of the war, just the southern region of the state alone would contribute around 17,000 aircraft to the United States military efforts. Seeing as the aircraft industry was growing rapidly in California, pilot training became commonplace, and the state sent over ten thousand pilots to aid the Allies in World War I. Thanks to the aircraft needs of the United States military during World War I, California's economy flourished in the 1910s. Hundreds of thousands of jobs were created, and Southern California, specifically Los Angeles and San Diego, cemented itself as one of the primary aircraft manufacturing locations in the United States.

California in the 1920s

While World War I helped boost California's economy during the 1910s, once the war was over, there was far less demand for the manufacturing of weapons, planes, and other military supplies. Factories and farms, which had expanded and hired thousands of extra workers, no longer had as large of demands, and many people were laid off as the companies attempted to downsize. The state's farmers, who had had massive demands during the war, were hit the hardest. That being said, the 1920s in the United States was a time of excessive spending. Over the course of the decade, automobile manufacturing became more commonplace, creating tens of thousands of jobs in the state as the demand for oil, street and highway construction, metals, and other automobile-related industries grew. The introduction of the car in the average American household is what would facilitate mass immigration to California over the course of the 1920s, as well as the following decades, seeing as settlers were no longer dependent on the railways. California's mass immigration came not only from within the United States but also from Asia, specifically the Philippines, during the 1920s. Although this boost in population and in tourism was encouraged during the twenties, as it became necessary for the growth of California's businesses and economy, it would become a matter of mass contention and dissatisfaction over the next decade when unemployment would reach an all-time high and Californians would feel their jobs were being stolen by immigrants.

Overall, the 1920s, in not only California but the rest of the United States as well, demonstrates exactly how divided the population truly was. While the twenties were a time of excess and partying for many, the rest of the population was socially and economically struggling. As the men returned from war and the farming sector of the economy suffered, the reunited families helped boost the urban population in California. Seeing as so many had returned from the horrors of war, the Roaring Twenties, as they are called, became about consumption, partying, and liberation for some. In the early 1900s, women had pushed for their right to vote, which they were finally granted in 1911. During World War I, women were granted another progressive liberty, the right to work, which became necessary as more and more men went off to war. Although women would not become common in the workforce until World War II, the 1910s and 1920s still represent a period of liberation for women of California and of the United States.

However, the twenties, which is often regarded as a period of liberation for many, was not a period of liberation for all. African Americans in California were considered to be second-class citizens, and although not officially segregated, African Americans, along with Native Americans, Mexicans, Chinese, and other racial minorities, were not allowed to attend white schools. While the civil rights movement grew in California, especially in Oakland, lynchings were still common occurrences, and Californians remained generally hostile to African Americans, even those who had fought alongside white American soldiers in World War I. Attitudes were not much better to the Asian population, and once again, the Asian minorities were resented for "stealing" Californian jobs, seeing as they were "willing" (forced) to work for less pay on farms. The racial tensions between California's Asian and white communities would continue to grow, especially in rural areas, which became apparent in the many violent clashes that would occur over the next decades, such as the 1936 Salinas Lettuce Strike.

The Great Depression

By 1940, the population of California would grow to 6,907,387, a growth of over four and a half million people from 1910. One of the greatest causes for mass immigration in the first few decades of the 20th century was the Great Depression. In October of 1929, on a day that has come to be known as Black Tuesday, the United States stock market crashed, affecting just about everyone in the country. People stopped buying products, businesses started laying off employees, families lost their homes, and while all this was happening, America endured one of its worst periods of drought at that point, another natural occurrence that northeasterners were not prepared for when they moved to California and other southern states. Californian farms suffered, and essentially all building and expansion projects were put on hold as the country tried to recover. Despite this, people continued to move to California. With idyllic movie scenes and paintings of the state in their minds, Americans flocked by the hundreds of thousands to hopefully find refuge in California. As seen in John Steinbeck's famous 1937 novel *Of Mice and Men* and his 1939 novel *The Grapes of Wrath*, immigrants arrived in California looking for work and essentially lived like nomads, moving from farm to farm as odd jobs arose.

However, as more and more immigrants arrived seeking a better life in California, the job market became smaller and smaller, especially since businesses continued to close down and lay off workers. Similar to their reaction to the Chinese laborers, the Californians quickly grew resentful of the American immigrants who were arriving in California and taking their jobs. In general, during the 20th century, California's class disparities became increasingly apparent as disasters occurred, such as the San Francisco earthquake or the Great Depression. By 1934, around a fifth of the population had to go on public relief to stay afloat. Immigrants continued to arrive, and since they were unestablished in the area, they were willing to migrate for jobs, which was not really a possibility for those who had established lives in California with families and homes. Once again, the percentage of the population who were homeless skyrocketed, and areas such as Oakland's Pipe City, where the unemployed lived in above-ground concrete sewer pipes, sprung up all over the state.

Political Reforms

After the disastrous events that plagued California's early history, such as the San Francisco earthquake and the Great Depression, the state's political system was put to the test and was eventually forced to change. Until the 20th century, California remained mostly relaxed about politics, seeing as the cities were mostly under the power of the businessmen. Californians seemed to share the common belief that "the best government was the least government." However, after the San Francisco earthquake, when the elite businessmen-run political parties failed the working class in the city, and when many civilians in California lost their jobs during the Great Depression, the state had an overwhelming need for a progressive and effective government. Although California had made some progressive political moves previously, such as the installation of the Workmen's Compensation, Insurance and Safety Act in 1913, the first real political reforms in California truly occurred in Washington, when President Franklin D. Roosevelt stepped in during the Great Depression and helped to regulate the economy. However, even with the installation of public relief, the population of California was not satisfied with their leaders, and the social unrest only grew with the arrival of immigrants taking Californian jobs during the Great Depression. Although the political unrest had been growing since the start of the century, the resentment culminated in the 1930s when violent worker protests and strikes broke out across the state, with one of the worst clashes being "Bloody Thursday," also known as the San Francisco General Strike of 1934.

Although there were protests and strikes by the unemployed, the employed population of California was not pleased with their conditions either. Those who did work worked excessively long hours in horrible conditions for poor pay, and during the Great Depression, employees had had enough and began to form and join unions to take action. The San Francisco General Strike of 1934 began after Harry Bridges, the founder and leader of the International Longshoremen's Association (ILA) labor union, led the dissatisfied workers in their labor strike on May 9th, 1934. This strike would inspire dozens of other large unions to gather along the Pacific coast and throughout the rest of California. After a little less than two months of striking, tensions escalated as the shipping companies refused to cooperate with the ILA's demands of better working conditions and wages. Finally, on July 5th, 1934, the dissatisfaction of the city of San Francisco, the striking members of the ILA, and the shipping companies culminated in a bloody clash, which would result in the injuries of dozens of men on both sides and the deaths of two. The event on July 5th, 1934, which came to be known as "Bloody Thursday," put an end to the ILA's strike, for the shipping companies gave in to their demands. The results of the ILA's strike inspired almost all of the employees in the San Francisco Bay Area to strike for their own rights, and the city was almost entirely shut down by striking employees for four days. The businesses in the Bay Area finally gave in to the requests of their employees, and the employees were aware that although their requests were met, working conditions during the Great Depression were still bad. As a result, they formed unions and threatened strikes when necessary.

Yet, despite the poor working conditions being slightly improved upon during the Great Depression, California's politics remained somewhat of a mess. Although the state was in disarray, millions were unemployed, and hundreds of thousands were homeless, Californian leaders somewhat frivolously spent the state's money to put California on the global map and set up the state's economy for the future. In 1932, the city of Los Angeles held the Olympics in its stadium, which had been built in the previous decade. The over-the-top Olympics celebrations that we know of today are accredited to being birthed in the 1932 Los Angeles Olympics, where the city set the present-day standard for the opening ceremonies, extensive facilities for the athletes, and the entire artistry of the event. In the words of journalist Westbrook Pegler, "I came to chronicle sports biggest disaster, I am leaving to describe its greatest triumph." The following year, the construction began on the San Francisco-Oakland Bay Bridge and the iconic Golden Gate Bridge. Over the course of the 1930s, a number of California's most important and iconic infrastructures were constructed, including the iconic Coit Tower and the Hoover Dam. The latter would not only provide clean drinking water but also allow the state to harvest hydroelectric energy.

Although the country looked up to Presidents Herbert Hoover, to some degree, and Franklin D. Roosevelt during and after the years of the Great Depression, Californians had no political force within their own state to look to for relief during the difficult years. While the Democratic Party improved its standing in the state over the course of the early 20th century, the Republican Party was still by far the popular choice; some of this may be attributed to the parties slowly changing platforms over the years. In 1930, the state elected Republican James Rolph Jr. (known as "Sunny Jim") as governor of California, and although he had served as the mayor of San Francisco during the years of 1912 to 1931, he was not at all prepared for his role as the state's leader during the country's worst economic period to date. Governor Rolph quickly lost popularity, and by the end of the decade, California would elect its first Democratic governor of the 20th century. Following James Rolph's successor, Frank Merriam, until the present day, the position of governor of California would swing back and forth between Republican and Democratic candidates. As of this writing, ever since James Rolph, California has not had three separate governors from the same party in a row, which just showcases the instability of California's politics, something that truly began during the Great Depression.

Overall, the state of California was in a strange state of affairs at the start of the 20th century. After years of mass immigration following the expansion of the railroads, the state endured a number of social and natural disasters, which left the civilians in a state of disorder. Although the working class, specifically the minority working class, in California never had it easy, the disparity between the rich elite and the poor working class became more and more apparent, and the public resentment finally culminated through strikes and riots.

World War II

When World War II began in 1939, the United States was reluctant to enter, seeing as they were still suffering from the effects of the Great Depression and it had not been long since World War I. This was especially true in California, which had become somewhat of a sleepy state, with unemployment at an all-time high. However, gradually, it seemed that the United States joining the war was all but inevitable. Still, Californians were reluctant to join yet again another devastating war, but this attitude would change on December 7th, 1941, due to the attack on Pearl Harbor. Seeing as Pearl Harbor was only around 2,500 miles away from Los Angeles, the people of California felt the urge to protect their country and family, and over the course of the next months, California became a fully-fledged participant in the Ally war efforts. Just as the Gold Rush had been close to a century ago, World War II was a wake-up call for California's population and economy. Similar to its reaction during World War I, California focused much of its attention on airplane manufacturing, although other weaponry manufacturing industries opened in the state as well. Farms, factories, and shipyards expanded and were suddenly in need of thousands of laborers, which very quickly put an end to the high rates of unemployment that had plagued the state and the country since the Great Depression. Although more than 800,000 Californian men would join the United States military and fight overseas, millions would be trained in Californian military institutions, meaning that, once again, the state's main contribution to the war would not be in men but in supplies, training facilities, food, and weaponry.

Although World War I had created California's aircraft industry, there had been almost no demand for Californian aircraft during the Great Depression. The start of World War II would force monumental growth in the industry. Californians designed, manufactured, and assembled everything from large bomber planes to small, fast fighter planes, injecting millions of dollars into the previously struggling economy. Alongside the aircraft industry, general technological advancements were made, such as radar, radio, and computer development, which would give birth to the state's soon-to-explode technological industry. On top of technology, the war gave a boost to the state's fields and farms, which had essentially died out during the previous decade. By the end of the war, California would actually contribute more food and other general war supplies (weapons, tech, aircraft, etc.) to the United States and Ally military than any other state in the country.

During the war, as the need for employees grew in the ever-growing aircraft, farming, and weapon manufacturing industries, the positions would not only be filled by the state's women but also by over a million Americans who had quickly immigrated to California in search of employment. Although California's population had been growing since the Gold Rush, there would be no greater boost in population since the Gold Rush than during World War II. Between 1940 and 1942, the state's population would increase by nearly a million people, and by 1950, the total population had grown to 10,677,000, an increase of more than 3.7 million people within the decade. World War II essentially skyrocketed the state's advancement toward the future, advancing its farming industry and shifting its economy toward technology development and manufacturing.

World War II represented a time of many social struggles and reforms for the various groups in California. Likely the group most affected by the Second World War was the Japanese, who represented quite a small population in California in the 1940s. The Japanese population had arrived in California mostly during the start of the 20th century to replace the Chinese on farms when anti-Chinese rhetoric became increasingly popular. Similar to the Chinese, the Japanese laborers had experienced prejudice and resentment from white Californians unable to find work during the early 20th century. However, hostility toward the Japanese

Americans truly worsened at the start of the Second World War when Japan sided with the Axis. Following the Japanese attack on Pearl Harbor, Americans' opinion toward the Japanese people worsened, mostly due to media fear-mongering, and by the end of World War II, the United States had imprisoned around 112,000 Japanese Americans, many of whom had been living in the country for many decades. The prisoners were not only men but also women and children as well, and seeing as California contained around 74 percent of the Japanese population in the United States, most of the internment camps were located in the state of California itself. Following the events of Pearl Harbor, it would take decades until the intense fearful American racism against the Japanese Americans would lighten, and the United States would not actually issue an apology for its treatment of Japanese Americans during World War II until the 1980s. Within the 1940s, the Japanese American population in California would decrease by more than 10,000, and the Japanese would not feel safe enough to return to California until the following decade.

Another group who faced racism in California during the Second World War was the African Americans, many of whom had migrated to California as the state's industries boomed and the need for laborers was in demand. Although prejudice in California was not as pervasive as in other southern states in America, the black population in California was still subjected to serious racism, segregation, prejudice, and violence. The conditions the African American population was forced to endure through the war would inspire much of the civil rights movement, which would gain momentum over the next decade.

While many racial minorities continued to experience racism over the course of the Second World War, other groups managed to achieve social reforms and gain liberties. Similar to during World War I, with masses of Californian men joining the military in World War II, women were allowed and encouraged to join the workforce. During World War II, women took up jobs in the various expanding industries. However, once again, just as it had in World War I, the reforms would only last so long. When the men returned from war, women who had helped to carry the country's economy during the soldiers' absence were encouraged to quit their jobs and return to being traditional housewives, which would help fuel feminism and the women's rights movement, which would grow astronomically over the subsequent decades.

The Effects of World War II

In 1945, the war came to a close, and although 26,019 Californians who served in World War II had lost their lives, over 800,000 returned home, tired and in need of rehabilitation. By 1947, more than half of the veterans, or GIs as they came to be known, were still unemployed, and alongside hundreds of thousands more, they claimed unemployment benefits to stay afloat. Although California's market had been massively helped by the Second World War, which helped the state recover from the effects of the Great Depression, California had the second highest veteran unemployment rate in the United States. Despite the struggles veterans faced upon their return to California, they were much better off than soldiers who had returned from battles before the Second World War. This was due to the 1944 GI Bill of Rights. The GI Bill not only aided veterans (GIs) who were unemployed but also helped them find and pay for homes and land, medical attention, and education. With the GI Bill encouraging veterans to return to school, Californian post-secondary schools, which at that point had not been well established, saw massive growth in students, which allowed the universities and colleges to build larger campuses throughout California.

California's veterans were not the only ones who struggled to find employment during the 1950s. Though World War II helped grow the state's economy, once it was over and the demands for tech, aircraft, and manufacturing were no longer as urgent, the

Californian economy entered into a period of depression. The year after the war had ended, California's unemployment rate was just under 9 percent, which was incredibly high in comparison to the United States' average of 3.9 percent. Overall, the main reason for the high unemployment rate was the constant growth in California's population over the course of the 20th century, which had not stopped in the years during or after the Second World War. Between 1945 and 1950, California's population would grow by more than one million people, meaning from the start of the war in 1939 to 1950, California's population increased by nearly four million people. Some of this immigration was due to the fact that millions of soldiers returned to the United States through California's de-embarkation centers. The United Nations also first met in San Francisco at the Opera House. This allowed thousands upon thousands of veterans to get a taste of California, many of whom would promptly decide to make the state their home. Overall, there were just not enough jobs for the ever-growing population, as well as for the returning military and the women who had been employed during World War II, some of whom wanted to keep their jobs.

Despite the first few years after the war being rather shaky for Californians, both those who had remained in the state and those who had recently returned, the economy quickly recovered and adjusted to the United States entering the Cold War. The effects of the Second World War were comparable to those of the Gold Rush. Throughout the late 1940s and 1950s, the economy continued to establish itself and prosper, while the population gradually grew, which brought upon a number of social movements, reforms, and changes.

California in the 1950s

In the words of Earl Warren, who was the governor of California between 1943 to 1953, "The war has caused us to actually jump into our future." Although California's wartime industries had very low demand in the first years following the Second World War, by 1947, America's need for weaponry, technology, and aircraft returned as the country entered the Cold War. By the end of the 1950s, more than three million people in the state worked in jobs related to Cold War defense, and Southern California became the United States' number one aircraft manufacturer.

During the 1950s, jobs were not as much of an issue as homes, which the state was seriously lacking in. Until this point, the urban population was entirely concentrated in a few cities, so the rural regions of California remained mostly undeveloped. However, this would no longer do for California's massive population. In the years following World War II, California's cities sprawled outward in all directions in a way they had not before, and the city suburbs, lined with simple, quick-built homes, were created to accommodate the masses looking to settle. Alongside the creation of the suburbs came the creation of the middle class, which had previously existed in California; however, for the most part, California was mostly split into the poor and the elite rich until the end of the Second World War. Although the middle class prospered in the suburbs, the vast majority of the working middle class were still employed in the cities, meaning they needed a stable form of transportation to get to and from work every day. Thus, in the 1950s, automobile ownership skyrocketed, as did consumerism in general. Middle-class families spent excessively on products that they could not have ever dreamed of owning before the war, such as dishwashers. By the 1960s, over 80 percent of the United States population owned a television, which had been a luxury item in the decades following its creation. As the middle class consumed, California's economy prospered, and the hundreds of new factories in the newly created product-manufacturing industries created jobs in the city for the unemployed. Thus, it became common for the poorer civilians in the United States to flock toward the cities from the rural areas, where the majority of the lower class had previously lived. Living in the city meant cars were not necessary, jobs were available, and homes were older and therefore cheaper. As the urban population sprawled into the suburbs, the newly settled middle-class population sought jobs, schools, shopping areas, and, of course, roads, in and around their immediate area, which also boosted the construction materials industry and construction employment sector. Overall, the state's economy not only recovered within the years following the Second World War but also grew astronomically, making California one of the wealthiest states in the country and one of the wealthiest regions in the world.

However, once again, this image of California's successes in the years subsequent to World War II fails to include the entirety of the state, and although the state of California did get wealthier, this wealth really only reached those who already had privileges before the war began. While it is true that over a third of California's women were employed in the decade following the Second World War, this was not, for the most part, because women wanted to be employed but because they were from a poorer family that could not live off the wage of the husband alone. This was especially common for recent immigrants and racial minorities, who struggled to achieve upward mobility amongst white Americans. One group who suffered from this was the Latin American population. As California's economy exploded in the 1950s, both the rich and the poor flocked away from the rural areas, where farms were still in need of workers. This led the United States to create the Bracero Program, which encouraged and facilitated over 200,000 Latin Americans, mostly from Mexico, to move to the United States and work on the farms, which generally offered lower and less secure pay than the booming industries in the cities. On top of only having work seasonally and working long hours for little pay, the Latin Americans were met with prejudice, discrimination, and sometimes violence from Californian farm owners, who knew they could get away with just about anything as the laborers needed the work. Although the Bracero Program ended in 1964, there are still to this day hundreds of thousands of Latin American laborers being underpaid and mistreated on Californian and American farms. Although the Latin Americans who arrived through the Bracero Program helped reestablish and fuel California's farming industry, they were not technically citizens of California, and if the growing season was poor and the farm needed fewer laborers that year, the Latin Americans, who had often established themselves in California with their working visas, were forced to return to their previous home. The laborers who wanted to stay in California could obtain a visa after having worked in the state for a set amount of years, but the road to obtaining a visa was difficult, and even if they earned citizenship, upward mobility was just as difficult.

The situation was also still difficult for the African American community in California, although it was improving. In the 1950s, the civil rights movement, with Martin Luther King Jr. as one of its figureheads, started making progress in improving the situation for every racial minority in all of America. Over the course of the mid-1950s, there were boycotts, rallies, and protests that finally called attention to the need for change. Although Mexican Americans had begun to desegregate Californian schools back in the 1940s, it would not be until 1955 that the United States would officially vote to desegregate schools. The desegregation of the housing market soon followed, allowing African Americans and other racial minorities in California and the rest of the United States to have the chance to purchase property in up-and-coming areas, attend better schools, and move upward in society, which had been almost entirely limited by government restrictions until that point. Although the years following the war were not great for all, many groups, including racial minorities, the LGBTQ community, and women, who had all previously suffered in California, began to make strides toward earning some liberties and respect.

Social Reforms in the 1960s and 1970s

If the 1950s in California represented a period of astronomical economic growth and the beginning of social reforms, the 1960s and 1970s represented a period of astronomical social change and development. Until the 1930s, California had been almost entirely Republican, and even as racial minorities immigrated to the state and social reforms were set in motion, the population remained quite traditional and right-leaning in their opinions. Though California would vote in its first Democratic governor in 1939 and numerous liberation movements would take shape in the years during and after the Second World War, it would not be until the 1960s that the state would become more left-leaning and Democratic. It would not be until the 1990s that California would become mainly Democratic, and it remains so to this day. In many ways, these political changes had been brewing since the dawn of the 20th century, yet the true breeding ground of the left-leaning ideas, which would be spread throughout the state over the course of the next decades, was California's post-secondary schools. During the 20th century, the percentage of the population who had or planned to attend university or college increased dramatically, especially thanks to the educational financial aid granted to soldiers who returned from World War II. Until the 1960s, higher education was mostly reserved for those who had the privilege to go, but that was about to change. In the 1960s, the postwar children who had been born in the homes of the suburban middle class had become young adults, and with the privilege of not having to work, university became a common next step for all twenty-something-year-olds looking to meet people their age rather than a luxury for those looking to join the workforce or seeking to expand their education. Quickly, California's universities had evolved to become a place to meet friends, party, join clubs, and, perhaps most of all, expand one's mind to the social reforms needed to make the country a better place for everyone. In the 1960s, at almost all of the California universities but most notably at the University of

California at Berkeley, students shared and spread liberal left-leaning ideas, which led to student demonstrations. Over the course of the 1960s and 1970s, UC Berkeley and other California universities would be a leading force in the civil rights movement, the free speech movement, and the women's rights movement. They engaged in LGBTQ and Vietnam War protests, rallies, and demonstrations as well, helping to set in motion numerous social reforms and spread liberal ideas throughout the state.

The universities in California also helped set the precedent of the United States' budding cultural movements. In the years following World War II, California would become an epicenter of almost every cultural movement. Los Angeles developed into not only a city for films but also for music, and the city helped establish many musical icons. San Francisco would have its famous Summer of Love, a hippie movement, which forced the country to reflect on its attitude toward relationships, drugs, and art. In the 1960s and 1970s, California inherited close to eight million immigrants who arrived from all over the world, but unlike in the past, people were not arriving to strike it rich or buy property and start a new life. Instead, people were arriving to join in on the cultural movements that were taking place.

California in the 1980s and 1990s

The population growth brought by California's social movements in the 1960s and 1970s, which carried on into the 1980s, was especially obvious in the smaller Californian cities with universities. Students arrived from all over the country to study in California's universities, which had become somewhat of a dream for politically interested and liberal-minded students, many of which remained in the state after graduating. San Diego, which in 1950 had a population of only 333,865, ended up receiving a large portion of the college graduates, and the population grew to over a million people by 1990.

The 1980s would also represent a period of many social reforms for nearly every group in California, much of which had been brought on by the work of the students from the 1960s and 1970s. In the 1980s, for the first time in many years, the Native American population in California would significantly increase, as would the populations of almost all of the state's ethnic minorities due to the increase of foreign immigration. As California earned its left-leaning, liberal reputation, millions flocked to the open-minded cities. This can be seen, for example, in San Francisco with the growth of the LGBTQ community, as this city quickly became known as the most gay-friendly city in America.

Yet, even though the end of the 20th century would mark California's most accepting, aware, and open-minded period to date, things were far from solved. Despite all of the successes by the various movements in the 1960s and 1970s, the state's prejudice problems were not solved, and racism continued, resulting in violent protests and rallies. The LGBTQ community also suffered during the 1980s and 1990s, but their primary issue was no longer discrimination and violence but AIDS, which would not only kill thousands of young LGBTQ people but also hurt the LGBTQ's reputation, as civilians became fearful of them.

California's technological industry, which had essentially been created during World War II, boomed during the 1980s' digital revolution. By the 1980s, California's businesses had almost entirely relocated from San Francisco to Southern California. That being said, Northern California's budding Silicon Valley, located around San Jose, would soon become the tech and start-up capital of the United States. However, after years of almost entirely uninterrupted economic growth, the late 1980s and early 1990s would mark the state's first financial recession since the period right after World War II. This financial recession actually affected much of the world, but there were two main reasons for the fiscal issues in California. Firstly, during the 1980s and 1990s, the state was plagued with droughts and other natural disasters, which impacted farming. Secondly, in 1991, the United States officially put an end to the Cold War, which meant California's tech, aircraft, and weaponry manufacturing industries were far less in demand.

Similar to the small recession that had occurred just after World War II, California recovered rather quickly from the 1980–1990 recession, and the years following the recession would represent massive accelerated growth in many industries and the state's economy as a whole. The main reason for California's quick recovery in the 1990s was the insane explosion in the world's high-technology sector, for which Silicon Valley very quickly became the hub. Although Silicon Valley had already established itself as a contender in the country's technological race with the inventions of the microchip by Intel in 1971 and the PC by Apple in 1977, its growth over the course of the 1990s would be unparalleled. This was mainly due to the widespread growth of the internet in the 1990s and the immigration of highly specialized foreigners who wanted to join in on the technological advancements in Silicon Valley. Silicon Valley would also become known as the capital of start-ups, as innovative, creative people moved to the area to start their companies. Silicon Valley would eventually hold most of the country's most notable and affluent companies, and present-day Silicon Valley contains Apple, Adobe, Facebook, Netflix, PayPal, and Tesla, to name a few. Thousands arrived in Silicon Valley, hoping to finance their next big idea, and investors, hoping to purchase a percentage of what could possibly become the next biggest company in the world, were more than willing to secure million-dollar contracts.

Chapter 10 – Present-Day California (2000–2021)

California's Economy in the 21ˢᵗ Century

The internet brought Silicon Valley, California, and the United States dramatic economic growth, similar to that of the Gold Rush, as the Nasdaq stock market index close to quadrupled in five years. Finally, after more than a decade of unprecedented growth, the stock market bubble burst in late 2002 and brought down hundreds if not thousands of the companies that had been started in California's Silicon Valley. At the start of the 21ˢᵗ century, California's economy was also plagued by the effects of 9/11 and energy issues that caused rolling blackouts, negatively impacting almost all of California's businesses. As it had before, California would rebuild its economy once again in the new millennium and establish itself as one of the most prosperous states in the United States. Although it would be affected by various global recessions, such as the one in 2008, California has maintained its position as the state with the highest GDP (gross domestic product) in the nation. That being said, by the 21ˢᵗ century, the division between the upper class and the middle and lower classes, which had always existed in California, had exponentially expanded. Although

California is one of the richest states in the nation, the wealth is not distributed, and it is held almost entirely by the elites in the society, such as the Silicon Valley businessmen and the Hollywood Hills celebrities. In fact, California has one of the highest homeless populations in the United States.

California's Politics in the 21st Century

In 2003, Californians voted Arnold Schwarzenegger as their state governor, and although Schwarzenegger was not the first actor or celebrity in politics (most notably preceding him was President Ronald Reagan), he was certainly a controversial pick. Even before Arnold Schwarzenegger was elected, much like Donald Trump, he had earned his place as a controversial celebrity with views that went against the liberal and Democratic scene in Hollywood. To many, Schwarzenegger represented a period of social regression, as he imposed laws that many felt directly hurt minority groups, such as when he and the California Supreme Court banned same-sex marriage in 2008. Overall, California is still far from perfect, and socially, it still has a way to go, but the state is considered to be far more accepting toward minority groups than other states in America. Following Schwarzenegger's terms, there has not been another Republican governor in California, as the state has become Democratic-leaning, which it had been gearing to become since the 1960s and 1970s.

Conclusion

California's development has always been completely dependent on its mass immigrations, which began with the forty-niners during the Gold Rush. As people came from all over the world to experience what they had heard about, read about, and eventually seen in the movies, few wanted to leave California's mild climate and beautiful landscapes. This was true during all of the mass immigrations surrounding the Gold Rush, the Great Depression, and World War II. Although the mass immigrations allowed California's economy to grow astronomically in only a few centuries, they were not without their problems. The state of California had long been inhabited by the first settlers of the region, who were continuously pushed out of their home as immigrants arrived. In fact, many native Californian tribes were actually relocated off of their ancestral land and out of the state entirely. Aside from the native Californians, the mass immigrants brought foreigners from just about everywhere, such as Asia, the United States, South America, Europe, and more. Yet, despite the fact that California was stolen from the Native Americans, many of the groups who arrived over the course of the most recent centuries felt entitled to the land. At first, the Spanish caused the Native Americans to suffer. When the Republic of Mexico acquired Mexico, both the Native Americans and the Spanish suffered. When the United States acquired Mexico, all three of those groups suffered. During the Gold Rush, California received its first mass immigration, and although foreigners arrived from all over the world to try and strike it rich, the racial minorities, including the Mexicans and Native Americans, who had lived in California long before the Gold Rush, were resented by the white newcomers, as were other racial minorities, most notably the Asians, who arrived at the same time. With California's mass immigrations would come mass entitlement, resentment, and social issues.

For many years, California remained quite similar to the other southern states, as it was quite traditional, segregated, and right-leaning by today's standards. However, over time, the racial minorities began to make up a majority, and before long, public opinion started to shift. With the widespread growth of universities and other post-secondary education schools in the 1960s and 1970s came the mass spread of information, and before long, California's universities became the home to almost every left-leaning social movement in the country. Students fought for women, LGBTQ, African American, and Asian rights, as well as many other issues. By the end of the 20th century, California had become a left-leaning state, and it eventually transitioned into the state we recognize today, a predominantly Democratic liberal population. However, it still has many issues to face. For example, present-day California is the most populous and wealthy state in the country, yet the wealth is only in the hands of a select few, and the wealth gap and social prejudices are still very much in existence. Only time will tell if California continues to embrace its current liberal stance or if it will switch to a more conservative outlook, a pattern that can be seen throughout the state's history.

Part 2: The California Gold Rush

A Captivating Guide to One of the Most Significant Events in the History of the United States of America and Its Impact on Native American Tribes

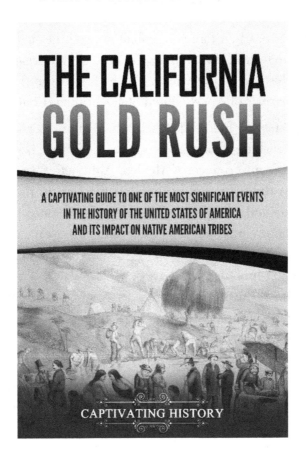

Introduction

In January 1848, when James Marshall noticed the first glimmer of gold at the bottom of the millrace, he didn't even dream he would change the history of the world. He had discovered gold at the bottom of the river of a new United States frontier, California.

In the years that followed, the newly acquired territory swelled with people rushing to make a fortune. California had previously been under the governance of Mexico. Although it was known that the Mexicans did some gold mining in the region, the European-Americans needed a bigger motivation to start settling in California. This motivation was provided by the discovery of gold, as newspapers rushed to exaggerate, promising that the gold was there for the taking. Only then did tens of thousands of people set on a journey to the West. But it wasn't only Americans who were struck with gold fever. Many miners came from Great Britain, China, Australia, South America, and other countries from around the world.

During the early years of the California Gold Rush, most of the people headed directly to the rivers. These first brave men and women are remembered in history as the forty-niners or the Argonauts, and there are many tales about their heroism, their struggles to settle in the wild western territories, and their troubles with the Native Americans. However, all these stories are heavily romanticized, and they do not tell historical events from an objective perspective.

The romantic stories of the Gold Rush pioneers disregard the violence, poverty, and famine that happened to the indigenous peoples of California. The arrival of European-Americans and Europeans sealed the fate of the Native Americans living in California. Even the US government approved mass killings and the relocations that followed. Although the period of the California Gold Rush is of extreme importance for the development of the United States of America, history should never tell a one-sided story. This is not only the tale of how the discovery of gold lifted the US to the top of the world's economies. This is also a story of society, laborers, the first immigrant laws, women and their role in the mining societies, slavery and freedom, and statehood. Finally, this is a story of genocide, of Native Americans who were forced to abandon their ancestral homes and relocate to designated reservations.

Chapter 1 – The Discovery of Gold

Gold panning

https://en.wikipedia.org/wiki/California_Gold_Rush#/media/
File:Gullgraver_1850_California.jpg

Only twenty years after the adoption of the Declaration of Independence in 1776, the United States expanded its territory and doubled its size. After another fifty years, the expansion reached across the plains, mountains, fields, and deserts, all the way to the Pacific coast. During the Mexican-American War (1846–1848), the US Army conquered the territory of Alta California, which allowed them to invade Baja California. When the war ended in 1848, California (among others) became a part of the United States under the terms set by the Treaty of Guadalupe Hidalgo. This expansion of US territory was President James K. Polk's vision, although many contemporaries criticized him for starting the war with Mexico. When Polk was near the end of his presidency, he addressed the nation on December 5th, 1848. He spoke of California, and the nation eagerly listened, waiting for the confirmation of the existence of gold. But what made the whole nation wait for such news? Why were they explicitly interested in hearing about California?

A single event occurred on January 24th, 1848. In the Sierra Nevada Hills, A carpenter from New Jersey, James W. Marshall, was building a water-driven sawmill when he found glittering gold in the river. At that time, Marshall wasn't sure what he found, and he thought it wise to consult his employer, a Swiss immigrant who had big dreams of starting a cattle farm in the new land. This immigrant's name was John Sutter (Johann Sutter), who came to California in 1839 after fleeing imprisonment in his home country due to unpaid debts. He became a Mexican citizen (at this time, California was a part of Mexico) and settled on a 48,000-acre ranch, which was granted to him by the Mexican government. In return, John Sutter promised he would curtail American efforts to take parts of California. He named this land New Helvetia, but instead of safeguarding the border against the American intrusions, he often helped the US migrants settle in the territory of Mexico.

When Sutter learned about the gold nugget his employee Marshall had found, he decided to test it. After all, he couldn't be sure if it was indeed gold. Together, Marshall and Sutter found information on how to test gold in an old encyclopedia. First, they pounded the golden nugget between two rocks. The nugget flattened but didn't break, a positive sign that they were holding gold. Then, they tested it in nitric acid, which would affect most metals except for gold. Still, they were not completely satisfied with the results, and they conducted one more test. They placed the nugget on a scale and counterweighted it with three silver coins. Then, they submerged the scales under the water. The side that contained the nugget sank, as gold had a higher density than silver. Finally, their suspicions were confirmed. They were sure they had found gold!

Their timing was very important, as this all happened only nine days before California became a part of the United States. Sutter was resolved to keep the discovery of gold quiet because he feared that his own cattle farm business would fail. He dreamed of building a farming empire, and the big influx of people that would come to mine the gold, as well as the landscape changes that would occur during the mining process, would bring down his industry. Sutter was right because once the Gold Rush began, his business suffered. But to prevent it, the first thing Sutter did was rush to confirm he owned the land on which the gold was found. Since California still belonged to Mexico, he had to file documents with the Mexican authorities. But the land he owned was on Coloma territory, and Mexico declined his claim on the land because, under the law, native peoples were not allowed to grant leases.

And even though Sutter tried, it was impossible to keep the news away from the public. A Mormon store owner and publisher named Samuel Brannan visited Sutter's Mill, and there, he acquired gold nuggets by trading with Sutter's Mormon workers. Upon his return to San Francisco, he started publishing news about his findings. But

Brannan was also the owner of a store in San Francisco and a visionary. He predicted the start of the Gold Rush, for which he pushed. He bought all the gold-searching equipment, such as picks, pans, and shovels, he could get his hands on. He would resell them for an enormous price while urging people to go to Sutter's land. In just nine weeks, Brannan earned more than $36,000. Taking into account the inflation rate since 1848, Brannan made approximately the equivalent of $1,200,000. He was the first person to become a millionaire from the California Gold Rush. But the rush hadn't yet started. People, in general, tended not to believe the journalists, especially the ones who settled in the new western territories. They believed that the claims about gold were just rumors.

While the journalist prospered, the Swiss entrepreneur Sutter suffered. The people rushed to his land and destroyed everything he had managed to build. The whole of San Francisco moved toward Sutter's farm. When the news hit Monterey, every soldier, sailor, and merchant was hit by gold fever. They, too, left for Sutter's land. Once there, they killed his cattle and burned buildings. Sutter lost everything except what little gold he had managed to find. Sutter managed to salvage some of his business and land, and he transferred the ownership to his eldest son. But the family lost their fortune, and their debt was increasing. Even though Sutter Junior started in Sacramento City in the vicinity of the family estate, he was forced to sell the land to pay off the debt. He then moved to Acapulco, Mexico. One of the businessmen who obtained this land was Samuel Brannan, the journalist who had started it all.

The people were already coming to California hoping to find gold, trusting the rumors of its discovery, before Polk's speech even took place. But the Gold Rush only truly began with his speech on December 5th, 1848. Polk explained that it was known that Mexicans had extracted gold in California before the territory was ceded to the US. However, the extent of the gold veins and their value and purity were unknown. The field reports Polk received from the public service officials who visited California during that year confirmed the abundance of gold. The whole nation listened and celebrated. The civilians were sure the gold was there for the taking, while the politicians congratulated Polk for adding California's gold deposits to the national inventory of natural resources. Even Polk's critics had to admit that the value of California was worth the war.

But, at first, even Polk was reluctant to trust the news of the discovery of gold. Three separate messengers were sent to him from California's military governor Richard Mason. One left on August 30th, 1848, by boat, through the Isthmus of Panama. This man arrived in Washington in November. The second one left on September 13th, and he traveled overland, crossing Mexico. He also arrived in Washington in November. The third and the fastest messenger was sent by land, but he managed to arrive in Washington on September 18th. It was only after receiving these three messages and three samples of gold that President Polk started believing in California's gold resources. The speech he held concerning California was just a spark, but the newspapers took over and exaggerated the stories, feeding the flame.

The *New York Herald* was the first publication on the East Coast to publish the discovery of gold in California. The people started rushing to the West in hopes of gaining wealth. San Francisco was only a small town of barely two hundred inhabitants when Samuel Brannan walked its streets, yelling, "Gold, gold in the rivers of America!" At the end of 1848, it already counted one thousand inhabitants, and over the next two years, it grew to house twenty-five thousand residents. In just four years after the announcement of the discovery, California's population increased from 14,000 to 250,000. But it wasn't only the number of inhabitants that changed almost overnight. It was also the composition of the population. Before California became a part of the United States, the majority of the population was Hispanic (around 80 percent). The Native Americans, who saw a decrease in their numbers over time, counted around 150,000 souls.

The population change had already started when California was ceded, as many people moved from the East Coast to the newly gained territory in hopes of gaining some land and starting farms. But it was not until the Gold Rush that the change in population composition started hurting the Hispanic and Native American populations. From 1849 until 1870, the Hispanics dropped from 80 percent to only 4 percent. Even though at that time California numbered around 380,000 people, only 31,000 were Native Americans. But it wasn't only US citizens who were rushing to California to extract its gold. There were many Chileans, Peruvians, French, British, Chinese, Japanese, and even Australians who were struck by the gold fever. Together with the Americans of the East Coast, they pushed the Native Americans from their land, away from their hunting grounds and natural resources. The new settlers brought diseases with them that Native Americans never experienced before. They had no immunity developed against them, and many of them succumbed to simple diseases such as the flu. But many more Native Americans were deprived of their land or killed.

When all the gold from the rivers was picked, and the only remaining sources were deep underground, mining became the only solution to acquiring gold. But to mine on the land that still belonged to Native Americans was impossible. So, the US government sought to remove the remaining native peoples. State legislature soon gave the new settlers in California the right to take custody of Native American children, thus effectively allowing slavery. Laws also gave the settlers the right to arrest Native Americans for any minor offenses, such as the possession of alcohol. The convicted natives had to work off their sentences. In the name of "protection," tens of thousands of natives were enslaved. Yet, this was just the beginning. The government wanted to resolve the "Indian problem" quickly, and they instigated hatred toward the native peoples. The settlers were convinced they couldn't get their hands on the gold before they removed the Native Americans, so they started slaughtering them. The government turned a blind eye to the violence and even started funding the local militias against the native tribes. Those Native Americans who tried to resist and fight back were poorly armed and had no experience in fighting with guns. They stood no chance against the whites. Local officials put bounties on Native American heads, urging the settlers to start massacres.

Chapter 2 – Going to California

Advertisement on sailing to California from 1850

https://en.wikipedia.org/wiki/California_Gold_Rush#/media/
File:California_Clipper_500.jpg

Before the Gold Rush, those who wanted to settle in the West would go toward Oregon's Willamette Valley. But after the discovery of gold at Sutter's sawmill, the Oregon Trail was changed forever. Thousands of wagons, carrying people, supplies, and equipment, poured into the Sierra Nevada, from where they would descend to Sacramento Valley. But in 1848, only around four hundred California-bound people were on this road. The very next year, that number climbed to thirty thousand. The Gold Rush pioneers were called "forty-niners" because they started their journey to California in 1849. Alternatively, they were called the "Argonauts," after the Greek myth about Jason and his ship, the *Argo*. In this myth, the heroes were chasing for the golden fleece of a magical ram, and with the help of the gods, they managed to find it.

But the road to the West was harsh, and the crowded paths became the resting place of many dead animals, discarded personal belongings, and wagon parts. Just in 1850, over two thousand wagons, horses, and mules were abandoned in the desert of California. One month after President Polk's speech, over sixty ships, filled with people eager to get to California, left the ports of the East Coast. Whaling ships were turned into passenger ships because the demand was so high that it was profitable to charge the people for transport rather than to hunt whales. But these ships were not well maintained for the most part, and they were in no condition to carry so many people. They sank before reaching San Francisco. Clipper ships, designed for speed, were the fastest, and they could reach California in only three months. But they were also the most expensive option. Time was money; the sooner you got to California, the more chances you had to find gold and to survive the hardship of the journey. The slowest were paddle-wheel steamer ships. They took almost a year to reach California. On average, a settler would travel for 115 days, starting in New York or Boston.

There were two sea routes to California. The first one went south from the East Coast, traveling the Atlantic to the Horn of Hope, around South America, reaching the Pacific, and then climbing north toward California. The second route went south to the Isthmus of Panama, where they had to then traverse the jungle with horses or mules for at least a week and catch a ship for California on the Pacific side of the Isthmus of Panama. The third route was completely by land, and it started at Independence, St. Joseph, or St. Louis, Missouri. The men would buy oxen and covered wagons, which they used to carry supplies and equipment. They would ride on horses next to the wagons. They also took passengers, who either occupied very limited space in the wagons or chose to walk next to the wagons. Traveling along the land route was very slow and exhausting. Some of them chose to turn south, which was known as the Santa Fe Trail. Then, they would turn toward California, the so-called Old Spanish Trail. Some forty-niners decided to take a boat to Texas, then ride or walk through Mexico to San Diego. This was known as the Sonora Trail.

Most of the people who were struck by the gold fever were poor, and to afford the trip to California, they had to sell everything they owned. Many of them even borrowed the money from their relatives, friends, or banks so they could pay for a ship ticket. They counted on getting rich from the gold they would find, which would allow them to pay off their debts. The average cost of the trip was around $1,000. But the minimum spending for the whole trip was around $750 per person. There were many dangers on the road, such as wild animals and bandits, so the Argonauts had to carry arms. They had at least a revolver and a knife, but rifles and shotguns were carried too. Some cases are known where walking sticks would turn into swords, batons, or blackjacks. The weapons also served hunting purposes or to shoot what little cattle the people brought with them. They were also used to protect one's claims to land and to shoot Native Americans, who would attack settlers on their way to the West.

But some of the biggest nuisances on the road to California were the robbers. Some were murderers, while others would take money and valuables but leave their victims alive. There were also thieves, gamblers, tricksters, and fraudsters. Some of them were even romanticized, and from their adventures, many legends have sprouted. The most famous legend is about Joaquin Murrieta. It is not known if he was a real person, as there is no firm evidence of his existence. There is one known case of horse theft committed by someone of that name but nothing else. The legend grew to immense proportions, and Joaquin became famous as California's Robin Hood. He wasn't simply a bandit but was on a path of revenge. He defeated all the Anglo settlers who accused him and his brother of horse theft and those who killed his young wife. According to the legend, the government had to put a bounty on his head, and Joaquin was eventually caught and killed.

Many people were killed on the road, some by robbers and Native Americans, but most died of various diseases. Cholera was the biggest problem. One traveler noted how in one day on the road, he would see at least four fresh graves. But the lives were also lost to hunger, accidental shooting, exposure to elements, thirst, various accidents, and much else. The landscape was hostile as well. One stretch of the road was named Death Valley by the Argonauts. Previously, this place was known as Tomesha ("ground afire" in the languages of Both the Paiute and Panamint Shoshone Native American tribes). The name is appropriate, as it is one of the hottest places on Earth, comparable to the Sahara Desert. In summer, temperatures in Death Valley reach up to 134°F (56.7°C). To avoid heat strokes and dehydration, forty-niners had to climb the nearby mountains where the temperatures were cooler.

The Argonauts hoped that a better life awaited them in California. But the scene that greeted them was a gloomy one. The hills around the city were filled with tents, as the overcrowding pushed people out of San Francisco. Overcrowding also brought the cholera epidemic to the city, as well as pest infestation. Hunger was also ever-present, mainly due to inflated prices. Merchants profited the most from the Gold Rush. The demand for goods rose because so many people flocked to California, and merchants increased prices as a result. The inflation was so high that it became ridiculous. A shovel, the most wanted tool of the Gold Rush, reached the price of $36. That is approximately $1,000 today. The food prices were similar. A pound of cheese (0.45 kilograms) would sell for $26 ($700 today), and a bag of flour was $13 ($365 today). The inflated prices also affected hotels, where a room for a night would go for $250 a week. Many chose to rent only a sleeping space, without bedding and with many people lying next to you. The price of such a sleeping space was $8. Land prices also went up. A lot that was 150 feet wide (46 meters) sold for $8,000. Only one year earlier, this land would cost $20.

In 1850, San Francisco had five hundred rotting ships abandoned in its bay. The passengers, crew, and captains had run off to search for gold. The resourcefulness of the people prevailed, and some of the ships were pulled onshore to serve as housing, prisons, churches, and banks. San Francisco workers earned a dollar an hour. In the East, they would earn that much in a whole day. But many of them were paid in gold dust because there was not enough money circling. Merchants would also accept gold dust as payment if a customer had no money. Coins were so rare that their value increased, and the miners ended up paying a whole ounce of gold (31.1 grams) for one silver dollar. The real price of that much gold was sixteen dollars.

Mining camps sprouted all over the flows of the Sacramento, American, and Feather Rivers. The names of the camps were descriptive and sometimes funny, with examples such as Whiskey Bar, Skunk Gulch, and Dry Diggins. Miners who came with the dreams of getting rich often lost their gold on bets. Finding gold also wasn't as easy as the people were led to believe. It is estimated that only one in five forty-niners would be lucky enough to find some gold. The rest had to go back home empty-handed. But the opportunity was there; it just needed to be found. Among the first Argonauts were the five prospectors of the Yuba River. In just three months, they made over $75,000. At Sonora, a lump of gold weighing 28 pounds (12.7 kilograms) was found. In the same area, eight more nuggets weighing more than 20 pounds (9 kilograms) were found. And at the Coloma sawmill, the workers found gold each day, and its worth was anywhere between $20 and $30.

The first phase of the California Gold Rush was collecting the gold nuggets from the shallow waters of the rivers. The first prospectors used placer mining methods, which included techniques such as panning. They would shovel the dirt from the riverbed into a "washing pan," swirl it around to wash the pebbles and gravel, and pour the water off. Because gold is denser, it would remain at the bottom of the pan. During the California Gold Rush, many people used this technique as their only method of extracting gold from the river. But if they tried to discover gold in deeper streams, they would have to use more sophisticated equipment, such as a cradle or a rocker. These devices were 3 feet (0.9 meters) long, with riffles inside them. One miner would pour gravel in the cradle, while the other one would rock it to wash out debris. The gold was trapped against the riffles. There was a larger device called the "long tom," which was a kind of sluice box that was at least over 6 feet (1.8 meters) long. The river dirt was shoveled at one end of the device so the water would wash debris away, allowing the gold to remain trapped.

The gold panning technique is old; it dates from ancient Roman times. However, it is believed that it was introduced in California in 1848 by Isaac Humphrey, a miner from Georgia. The Mexicans developed their own panning technique with a flat dish called batea, and they might have actually brought the technique to California first. Nevertheless, panning was the most used method of gold mining during the California Gold Rush. It was a very slow method. A skillful miner would wash out fifty pans of river gravel during a twelve-hour workday. Even then, he would be lucky to obtain a few small nuggets of gold. Isaac Humphrey is also credited with the introduction of the cradle to California. Miners were capable of processing more river gravel with the cradle than with a pan.

However, this device had its disadvantages, as it would fail to capture the smallest specks of gold in its riffles.

The easy pickings from the riverbeds ended in 1850. After that, there was simply no more gold to be found floating freely. What gold was left was locked in quartz deposits or were buried deep underground. When it came to the deposits, the miners resorted to building crushing mills. The quartz and rock had to be crumbled so that the gold could be extracted. But extraction wasn't simple. Mercury was used because it has the ability to trap gold. Then, the mercury would be melted and evaporated, leaving the gold free. These mercury vapors were poisonous, and gold extraction with this process was very dangerous.

Sometimes, the gold was simply too deep for common miners. They were unable to build or find the tools and equipment that could reach 50 feet (15.2 meters), as they were quite expensive. But if the gold vein was large, capitalists from the East would invest in the mines, and miners worked not for themselves but the investors. Soon, only big companies with expensive machines were left mining. They used huge dredges to sift through whole riverbeds, and they also used hydraulic mining techniques to force the water and gravel through narrow nozzles. Whole rivers, harbors, and farms were destroyed by this method of mining because large amounts of water, gravel, and dirt accumulated in the lowlands. Farmers were forced to move their cattle and fields or to fight the big corporations in courts so they could save their land.

The peak year of the California Gold Rush was 1852. In that year alone, companies excavated four million ounces (113,400 kilograms) of gold, which was worth eighty-one million dollars. The next year, they excavated seventy million dollars' worth of gold. But the amount of gold was declining, and between 1865 and 1885, they managed to earn between fifteen and twenty million dollars each year. The lowest amount was in 1900 when the mining companies earned only eleven million dollars. The largest amount of gold in

California was found in the Sierra Nevada region, known as the Sierra Nevada goldfields. From the beginning of the Gold Rush up until the late 1890s, approximately 20 million ounces (620 tons) of gold were excavated here. In the north, the gold was found at the site of today's Yreka in 1851. The whole region became known as the Northern California goldfields. In 1848, near Nashville in El Dorado County, the term "Mother Lode" was used for the first time. It refers to the rich veins of gold that run through the limited territorial area.

Chapter 3 – The Labor Force

Gold Miners in California in 1850

https://en.wikipedia.org/wiki/California_Gold_Rush#/media/
File:1850_Woman_and_Men_in_California_Gold_Rush.jpg

Free miners remained in California until at least 1873, which is astonishing. Other mining states were completely capitalized by big corporations as soon as minerals and precious metals were discovered, but in California, a free miner, a common man, was the backbone of the whole system. The importance of the common man can also be seen in the abundance of evidence that comes directly from them. They left behind diaries, letters, and memoirs, which tell the everyday stories of the miners' lives. There are also ship records, newspaper articles, and reports from governmental agencies, which testify that ordinary people came to California in great numbers. But social and labor history is often disregarded as irrelevant when it comes to the Gold Rush, as this era was romanticized by historians and everyday people. The miners were represented not as a labor force but as adventurers seeking a better future. This is not completely untrue, but it is also not the only aspect of the laborer's endeavors. Because of this, it is important to get into the details and explain who the people were who joined the California Gold Rush. It is also important to find out how they lived and worked and how gold fever generated nationalism.

In just two years, from 1848 to 1850, California gained 300,000 people. They were all individual prospectors seeking the nuggets of gold in the California rivers or business owners moving to take advantage of this newly discovered market. In 1850, 75 percent of California's population were miners. But that number drastically fell ten years later, as the miners made up only 38 percent of California's workforce. It can be understood why the news of the discovery of gold would attract those who were already in the mining business, but it remains to be explained why so many people felt the urge to go and try a profession they had never practiced before. The first to arrive in California were miners from the British Isles, as well as experienced workers who came from the silver mines of Chile, Mexico, and Peru. But these new immigrants were only a fraction of the population that rushed to California. They were soon followed by Americans who had participated in earlier gold rushes in North Carolina and Georgia. Still, professional miners remained a minority.

Historians often blame newspapers for creating the gold fever. Journalists were more than eager to exaggerate the news of the discovery of gold in California, promising a quick fortune for everyone. At the time, agriculture in the northeastern US was in decline due to the rapid industrialization of the nation. Farms were no longer needed in such large numbers, as production had developed in big factories in the American cities. The people were destined to either struggle on failing farms or accept working in textile or shoe factories for a dollar a day. Promises of fortunes in the West were just too pleasing. At the time, egalitarian republicanism was on the rise, and the single-minded pursuit of wealth was encouraged by the political scene of the 19th-century United States. No wonder many were ready to take on the adventure and settle in the new western frontier. As we said earlier, the Gold Rush appealed to the poor, and they came in great numbers. However, they were never the poorest of the poor. They owned enough or had a family to borrow from so they could pay for the journey to California. The abject poor remained in the East, as they had no chances of gathering the $300 needed for the cheapest route to the West.

But not all who rushed to the West were motivated by the promise of gold. Faith, as well as the recently coined Manifest Destiny, drove a substantial amount of people to seek new horizons. The church needed to establish itself in the new frontier, a territory that had only recently been obtained from the Mexicans. And the ardent nationalists who firmly believed in the doctrine of Manifest Destiny, which stated that America was a God-given land, rushed to bring democracy and capitalism across the entire country. Unfortunately, with the ideology of Manifest Destiny came nationalism, and it was often used to justify harsh actions toward groups that were not European-American.

Although people seeking wealth were independent entrepreneurs, they were often forced to cooperate to build dams, dig tunnels, and reroute river flows. But even then, their cooperation was short, and partnerships were sparse. The labor practices in California during the Gold Rush era consisted of individual labor, North American slavery, Latin American peonage, and Chinese indentured labor. Blacks were a minority when it came to free private miners. They came as free men, often taking the abandoned ships that were supposed to sail to New England. However, a greater number of them came as employees or slaves of the wealthier white gold-seekers. There are no records that would confirm their numbers, but it is estimated by scholars that, by 1850, around two thousand miners were African American. At least 50 percent of them were slaves. It is a similar story with the Mexicans, but it is known they were much higher in number, probably around fifteen thousand. We will never know how many followed their patrons and were part of the unfree labor force. The Mexican patrons encouraged the movement of the peons, and they financed their transportation to California. The same patron system brought an unknown number of miners from other Latin American countries, such as Peru and Chile.

The Chinese were among the last to arrive. In 1850, the whole United States numbered about one thousand Chinese, and only five hundred of them were miners. But this changed in 1852 when, in just that year alone, twenty thousand Chinese entered California. However, the majority of the new Chinese immigrants were not miners but merchants. These merchants were often able to pay for their journey to North America. However, the miners coming from China were poor and couldn't afford the journey. Nevertheless, they accepted the credit system that was put in place by "middlemen." These prospectors would finance a miner's journey to North America, and the indebted miner would pay him back over time with the riches he gained there.

With so many nationalities flocking to California, nationalism and xenophobia were on the rise. The reasons were many. Americans preferred to have others working for them for free. If the minorities worked for foreign mining companies, they were seen as taking jobs away from those who lived in the nation, and they needed to be expelled or at least work for the American-born miners. Another reason was that the American miners were aware that the quantity of and access to gold. They observed the success of experienced miners from Latin America, and they resented them for it. To add fuel to the fire, the Mexican-American War ended in victory for the US, which helped reinvigorate Manifest Destiny ideology. Many Americans presumed that they had more rights to the gold in California than the defeated Mexicans. This also led to some violence against Europeans and Australians but not as much as against the colored people groups. Racism, which was prevalent even when the Mexicans oversaw the land, rose, especially when free miners turned to paid labor during the 1860s. It was known that the foreigners would work for less money, which led to their resentment by the white workers.

Foreign miners felt discrimination in legal terms too. In the 1850s, two new taxes for foreigners were implemented by the state legislature. The first tax targeted only Mexicans, and they had to pay $20 per month for a license to mine. The tax led to ten thousand Mexican miners abandoning their work and leaving California. The American merchants lost a significant number of their customers, and they rose in protest against this tax in 1851, which led to its repeal. By 1852, the influx of Chinese miners led to the implementation of another tax. This time, the amount was set to $3 per month. Later, it was raised to $4, an amount the Chinese were willing to pay. The Native Americans were not a target of these taxes, but they suffered the most violence of all the minority groups. At first, they were seen as a labor force to be used, and in 1848, they represented half of the miners in California. But the conditions of their lives and the fact that they were not paid for their work but instead given rations testifies that they were an unfree labor force.

Life in the Digging Sites

In the early years of the California Gold Rush, the equality people felt and promoted came from the idea that everyone had the same opportunity to find gold. All one needed was luck. And this was true for those early days, as the majority of miners were individual prospectors and worked with simple tools. They also felt some level of unity because working together allowed them to build bigger devices and wash out more river gravel and debris than if they panned alone. For the most part, they all dressed the same, in simple and dirty mining clothes, which erased the class differences between them. Their outfit also often consisted of heavy boots, a checked shirt, sturdy trousers, gloves, and a large belt that could hold tools. Thus, even clothing played a role in shaping the miners' identity. They were workers, proud to earn their fortunes by their sweat and blood. They often resented other occupational groups, such as doctors, lawyers, and merchants, even though they often depended on them. They regarded themselves as hardworking people, while the other professions were there to exploit their willingness to endure hardship.

The miners who came to California between 1848 and 1849 were either individuals or came with their families. By 1850, when there was no more gold to be easily picked with simple panning, the miners formed companies of four to eight people. Together, they would build cradles, dams, and sluices in order to be able to process more river gravel than before. The work was not only hard but also uncomfortable. Although the sun would burn the workers, they had to work in ice-cold waters that had accumulated from the melting snows of the mountain tops. The miners would take a break during the hottest hours of the day, but the work generally lasted from 6 a.m. until the sunlight was gone. The work was also seasonal, as there was no searching for gold during the winter when the rivers were frozen. That means the miners also felt a sense of urgency. They needed to find enough gold to sustain them through winter.

They were able to wash 160 buckets of water every day to find one ounce of gold. However, the miners had the option to go south for the winter, where the dry mines were. But even there, the period of effective work was very short, as the rains and bad weather would come in the springtime.

Digging sites were almost completely devoid of women. Men were forced to both work and care for food and other domestic necessities. They learned how to wash, sew, and cook. However, many people never acquired these skills and instead hired domestic-related services in the mining towns. Even in larger mining towns, such as Grass Valley and Nevada City, only one in every ten men were married during the 1860s. Among miners, the number of married men was even lower, with one per every twenty-five. Even though the number of women in California was small, they had their own role to play during the Gold Rush era, which you can read about more in the next chapter.

A miner's diet often consisted of bread, meat, biscuits, and coffee. Fresh fruit and vegetables were rare. Although transport lines developed over time, domestic vegetables and fruits were the only ones the miners ate, and they were consumed for a very short seasonal period. Miners didn't lack food, but many of them still starved. This was due to price inflation. Also, with the dietary deficiencies and the lack of minerals and nutrients acquired from fresh food, people suffered diarrhea, scurvy, and dysentery. After 1850, the situation improved somewhat, as the development of large mining companies invested in better food transportation.

Other diseases quickly spread through the mining towns due to the hastily erected primitive houses, which were unclean and offered little protection from the elements. Most miners lived in canvas tents, but some built log cabins. After 1850, the mining towns began to be established, and the situation improved. But even then, these early towns were mostly made of rudimentary cabins. It was only after the 1870s that they started building proper brick houses.

But none of this stopped the movement of the miners. They worked for five months and then would retreat to cities such as Sacramento, San Francisco, or Stockton for the winter. The miners often needed to find jobs during the winter months because many of them had no luck in finding any gold. Even during the mining season, they would constantly move, trying to find spots rich with gold.

From Adventurers to Wage Laborers

The glory days of the forty-niners, Argonauts, and adventurers were short-lived. Those who caught the gold fever early, in 1849, were still able to make a fortune by collecting gold from the rivers of California. By 1850, their luck started to turn, and they had to lose their independence to survive. During the 1850s, the Argonauts worked as wage laborers for corporations that employed hundreds of people. At first, the corporations sought to attract experienced miners, and they targeted those who came from abroad, especially the British Isles. But very soon, in just a few years, they started employing anyone interested in trying their luck in finding gold. Of course, some of the first Argonauts were lucky and managed to get rich practically overnight. But most of them had no such luck, and they had to accept reality. To survive, they had to accept regular wages. Soon, they were working for similar prices and under similar conditions like factory workers in the East.

Because the companies sought to employ more and more miners, the wages dropped by half in just one year. The foreign experts were being paid $20 a day back in 1848 and 1849. But when the companies started employing just any forty-niner, the wages dropped to $10 a day. Three years later, the wage was $5, and in the late 1850s, it was only $3. The decline in wages mainly occurred because the cost of living started declining too. In the early 1860s, only one in ten miners owned some property. Merchants and businessmen, on the other hand, lived much better lives. For the most part, they owned their own properties and were family-oriented men.

Chapter 4 – Women in the California Gold Rush

Women in a brothel in San Francisco during the Gold Rush era

*https://en.wikipedia.org/wiki/Women_in_the_California_Gold_Rush#/
media/File:Early_San_Francisco_prostitutes.jpg*

Of all the immigrants who rushed from the East Coast to California during the early days of the Gold Rush, only 3 percent were women. The whole mythic and historical narrative of the California Gold Rush is oriented on men, their endeavors, adventures, and hardship. But women were, although in much smaller numbers, a contributing factor to the mining communities. They worked the goldfields alongside men, cared for children or the sick, maintained boarding houses, and entertained. Sometimes, they even earned more than their husbands. Women saw prospects in California and were attracted to a freedom that was impossible back in the East. Some were brave and adventurous, while others were gentle and caring. Women of all professions and races made up the diverse mining communities. They were pioneers, settlers, and pillars of family and society.

Women emigrants often wrote diaries and letters back home, and these are some of the best sources that historians have at their disposal in understanding the hardships people went through to reach the new frontier. From these writings, we can often learn how the mining communities lived and developed over time. Some of these women were even journalists, working for the newspapers back in the East. Their task was to follow men and report on life in California. But whether they were housewives, entertainers, or journalists, these women wrote eloquently, their writing sometimes filled with humor.

The first women to collect gold in California were Mexican and Native American women, as they were already there when the gold was first found. Many labored as slaves, although sometimes they were free women panning for gold alongside their families. Even children were involved in the search for gold, both boys and girls. These families were established in California long before it became a part of the US. Californian Mexicans were called Californios, and women played a very important social role in their communities. Once the Anglo-Americans and Europeans started arriving in

California, they sought to marry Californio women, as they realized they would open the door to the already established high society of California. Californio women didn't work the goldfields, but they were an integral part of the miners' lives. They were the mistresses of the estates, and they were respected and often romanticized.

The first wave of miners also brought the first major wave of Anglo-American women to California as early as 1849. Some of them simply couldn't let go of their husbands, and they decided to come along. Other women were struck by gold fever and wanted to take their own chances at creating their fortunes. Among the earliest women to arrive in California were the entertainers. They were dancers, singers, actresses, and prostitutes. They were well aware of the scarcity of women in California, and they wanted to capitalize on it. Most of them were already experienced in these lines of work, as they had worked in theaters, saloons, dance halls, or brothels in other cities and even other countries.

For instance, when the California gold fever hit France, many French miners came, but so did women, who were quickly employed in saloons to serve drinks or in gambling houses to rake the winnings. They were paid well, up to $250 a week. However, these women would quickly marry merchants or businessmen who brought their companies to California. The first French women were considered to be of "good character," as they rarely indulged in prostitution. But they were followed by a bigger company of ladies from France, which consisted of various characters. In 1850, the *Pacific News*, a newspaper from San Francisco, wrote that nine hundred French women were expected to arrive.

But French women were not the only ones to come. They may have been pioneers, but soon, ladies from all over the world started arriving. Most were Chilean, Peruvian, and Australian women who followed their husbands or came to work as prostitutes. They were the first to settle the mining towns near gold-bearing rivers, and they quickly prospered. One Anglo-American prostitute claimed she managed to earn $50,000 in just two months. But while these free women, for the most part, earned money by their own free will and choice, Native American women were seen as lower creatures, and they were often raped and passed around for free. Many of the other women didn't sympathize with the Native Americans. They mocked them and refused to help or treat them when they were injured or sick.

Enos Christman, a journalist and publisher from Pennsylvania who came to the goldfields in 1849, wrote how all the women he met had low morals, were constantly drunk, and served men's pleasure. He also wrote that meeting a good woman who was capable of reading and writing was almost impossible. He only personally met several ladies in California who were "good" and had families. He also claimed that all the foreign women who came to California were prostitutes. But Christman's words were not how other men felt about these first women. Miners actively sought the company of women, and they didn't consider them immoral.

During the early part of the Gold Rush era, there were no laws that regulated sex workers, and many madams were able to earn a fortune by opening and maintaining brothels. Most women who came to California during those early days had no money for the journey. Nevertheless, ships accepted them and expected them to pay for their trip upon arrival. This was no problem at all, as the saloons, brothels, and gambling halls gladly employed them and even paid their debt for the ship ticket. The girls would work off the price in three to six months. But ships also accepted women without money because they could advertise themselves as "having girls onboard" in order to attract male Argonauts to come and sail with them. Women were so valuable and scarce that men were willing to pay $20 just for the privilege to sit at the same table as the lady.

When it comes to the prostitutes in California, there was a hierarchy in terms of value. The fairer the skin they had, the more worthy they were deemed. Anglo-American, French, and other

European girls were highly sought, and they were the most expensive prostitutes, often reserved for wealthy businessmen. In popularity, Latino women came next, followed by the Chinese. Chinese women were at the bottom, but only because the Native American women weren't worth any money at all. Chinese women were also very rare, especially at the beginning of the Gold Rush era. By 1850, there were only seven of them in the whole San Francisco area. The first Chinese prostitute to arrive is believed to be the famous Ah Toy, who arrived in 1849. She initially sailed with her husband, but he died during the voyage, so she found herself completely alone in the new land. Luckily, she had some money saved, and she started her own brothel, importing girls from China, often as young as eleven. Ah Toy became famous not only for being the first Asian prostitute in California but also because she was brave and able to defend herself and her business from Anglo-American and Chinese men who sought to control her.

Women of good reputation came right after the "entertainers." Most of the women would take the Isthmus of Panama route, as it was the fastest and least dangerous. They traveled either with their husbands or in groups of other women who were also on their way to meet their husbands, who had settled in California at an earlier date. Some of them complained of the conditions of the journey, but they all displayed an iron will and a determination to finish their route. Some of them were fully independent and alone, struck by the gold fever themselves, hoping they could become miners and find their fortunes. Some women sailed around Cape Horn, but they were in the minority. Yet, we know about them, for we can see their names in the ship logs. The poorest, but also perhaps the bravest women, were those who crossed the land route to California. They were seldom alone, always accompanied by their husbands and children. Sometimes, though, their husbands were waiting for them in California, in which case it would just be the women and children. Some of them even dared to start a journey with babies. The stories from their diaries are sometimes hard to read, as they described the hardships of crossing Death Valley.

These women who crossed the plains in covered wagons had a lot to tell. Some of them were even celebrated as heroes because they were brave enough to stand by their men when their caravans were attacked by Native American tribes. They cared for the sick, buried the dead, and counted graves. Their diaries often describe how they had to leave oxen, horses, dogs, and sometimes even men behind in order to increase their chances of survival. Catherine Haun wrote of how her family had to abandon their dog, who was so exhausted from heat and thirst that he couldn't take another step. She later found out that the family who was traveling in a wagon behind them took the dog and ate it. Food was sparse, but water even more so.

Juliet Brier was one of the first women to cross Death Valley in 1849. She traveled with her husband, a reverend of the Methodist church who embarked on the journey to spread the faith to the West. The Brier family arrived in Salt Lake City too late in the season and couldn't cross the Sierra Nevada mountain range. They decided not to hesitate in Salt Lake City and instead continued west, taking an alternative road known as the Old Spanish Trail. But once they came to present-day Enterprise in Utah, they decided to split off from the main caravan and join a different group of one hundred wagons that were willing to try a route they had learned about from a passer-by. Allegedly, this was a shortcut and should have brought them to California much sooner. They followed a makeshift map that showed Walker Pass, but the map itself wasn't reliable. The Brier family and their party missed the mountain pass and continued walking west in what was to become the most horrible part of their journey, a desert with hardly any water sources and without a path for their wagons. They were forced to continue on foot, with some animals but no wagons. Most of the animals they had to kill and turn into jerky so they had enough food for the road ahead. Juliet was said to have done most of the work. She walked and carried her three children (all under eight years old) so they wouldn't slow down the party. She labored and cared for her family, and she was the only reason they all survived the horrors of Death Valley and made it to California. She nursed the sick, took care of the animals, and cooked. Other travelers remembered her as the "best man of their party."

Chapter 5 – The Golden State

San Francisco 1850/1851

https://en.wikipedia.org/wiki/California_Gold_Rush#/media/
File:SanFranciscoharbor1851c_sharp.jpg

When the United States acquired California from Mexico, it did not immediately become a state. But once gold was discovered, people began to flock in droves, and the citizens of California wanted to control their future. In these early days, California was administered by Congress, but it was unable to control the people, so a local government was needed to implement a system of law and order.

Even US President Zachary Taylor (served 1849–1850) urged the people to apply for statehood. By late 1849, the residents of California voted to become a state. But a major main question remained: What kind of a state would it be? A free state or a slave state? After all, over two thousand African Americans came to settle in California, and up until that point, they were considered to be free. Although racism was strong in the mining camps, some of them chose to stay. The majority settled in larger cities, where prejudice against them wasn't so obvious.

The Congress passionately debated about California's status, and in 1850, they came up with the Compromise of 1850. Finally, California could enter the Union as a free state. On September 9th, 1850, California officially became the thirty-first state of the United States of America. However, racism persisted even though California became one of the most progressive states in the US. For instance, Californios had been respected by the European-Americans when the territory belonged to Mexico. But now that it was a US territory, the Spanish-speaking people suffered heavy discrimination. Anyone with a darker shade of skin was perceived as unwanted. Besides having to pay foreign mining taxes, the Californios lost their ranches, as the European-Americans took them over and divided them into smaller farms. Mexicans were considered naturalized citizens, but that didn't matter; they were still forced to pay the foreign mining tax, just as anyone else coming to search for gold in the US. They also had to endure lynchings, beatings, and robberies. This all led to many Californios leaving the goldfields by the end of 1850 and going south to Mexico.

The Chinese were also discriminated against heavily. There weren't many of them during the initial years of the Gold Rush, but by the late 1850s, they numbered around twenty-five thousand. They spoke little English and were not Christians. This was enough for the European-Americans to think of them as suspicious and not trustworthy. The Chinese were often accused of stealing and of intentionally destroying campsites. In 1854, a proposal to keep the Chinese from arriving in the US was put forward, but it didn't pass. However, around twenty years later, Congress finally passed the law through which the immigration of some Chinese people was stopped. With the Page Act of 1875, Chinese women were banned from migrating to the US. This was the first-ever federal immigration law implemented in the United States. The intention was to stop the influx of cheap labor, but it targeted only women because they were thought to have loose morals. In 1882, a new law was implemented, the Chinese Exclusion Act, by which both men and women of China were banned from immigrating to the US.

But the Native Americans in California perhaps had the saddest fate. They numbered around 300,000 before the arrival of the European-Americans. The Chumash were the largest group, with over ten thousand members. Although the Native Americans who occupied California belonged to different tribes and were culturally and linguistically distinct from each other, they rarely engaged in tribal wars. Instead, they lived in peace, at least for the most part, and shared the land, with the different tribes adapting to living in different regions. When the first Spanish and Mexican missions came to California in 1769, they had but one goal: to introduce Christianity to the indigenous peoples. However, the Spanish rule was devastating for the Native Americans. During the Mexican regime, most tribes died out due to various diseases that had been imported from Europe. Violence was also not uncommon, and modern historians believe that these Christian missionaries treated natives as little more than slaves.

Once California became a state, the federal authorities essentially made the extermination of Native Americans legal. They even financed it, and many settlers, miners, and farmers joined in. When the news of the extermination of Native Americans reached other parts of the world, there was no reaction. In fact, in 1850, the California authorities came up with the Act for the Government and

Protection of Indians by which the white settlers could legally take Native American children from their parents. The intention was to apprentice these children and integrate them into American society. In reality, they were used as free labor. Children were not the only ones who were forced to work for free either. Around twenty-seven thousand adult natives labored for free, as they had no money to pay the alleged bonds or bails for crimes that they often didn't commit. Even though California was a free state on paper, what they did to the Native Americans is considered a form of legalized slavery.

Most of the Native American deaths were recorded between 1846 and 1873. More than 370 massacres took place during this period. Men, women, and children were killed by death squads that were formed from local militias and financed by the state. But the first two years of the California Gold Rush were the hardest. More than 100,000 Native Americans were killed or chased away from their land. Some of them tried emigrating to the north, but there are no records of what happened to them. The US government approved and financed more than 1,500 raids on Native Americans. To avoid mass killings, some tribes agreed to relocate to reservations. This was the fate of the Yokut tribe that inhabited the area around the Fresno River. But many tribes refused to be taken away from their land. The Yosemite tribe persisted the longest, as they inhabited the territory of what is today known as Yosemite National Park for centuries. But when the government captured the Yosemite chieftain in 1851 and killed his son, he finally agreed to sign a treaty and bring his people out of the mountains to the reservation dedicated to them.

The first apology for these crimes against humanity that had been committed in California during the 19th century came from California Governor Gavin Newsom. In 2019, he proclaimed that the massacres that took place were indeed genocide and that they should be described as such in history books.

However, the Native Americans were not only legally persecuted and killed; they also suffered the loss of their land. The ecological impact of mining is not to be underestimated. The Native Americans mainly thrived as hunters and gatherers. They lived in nature, and the environment was incredibly important for their survival. Due to the excessive mining, the landscape of the Sierra Nevada changed. Toxic waste was released into the rivers, killing fish. The animals that Native Americans depended on, such as buffalos, deer, and rabbits, disappeared from the region, which led to starvation.

Chapter 6 – The Significance of the California Gold Rush on the Global Economy

The timing of the discovery of gold in California is probably what propelled the United States to become one of the driving economic forces in the world. For most people, the mention of January 24th, 1848, means nothing; the date itself is not even commemorated in the state. However, that is when it is thought James Marshall found his first gold nugget in California, setting the stage for great events to happen. At the same time, the American nation was about to feel the impact of growing industrialization. The Industrial Revolution was already happening in Europe, and it moved its way toward the fairly new country, transforming it from an agrarian society into an industrial giant.

Looking at the larger picture, one can see the California Gold Rush was crucial for triggering economic changes in the country. Because of the large influx of gold, the US economy significantly accelerated. The result was the creation of new businesses and banks, as well as new governmental financial institutions. Agricultural expansion was stimulated too, and the volume of trade and commerce grew. New forms of transportation were also needed, which only served to further boost industries.

The Gold Rush moved many people across the US, but not all of them were miners or adventurers who sought to turn their luck by finding gold. Many of them rushed to California to start new business ventures or open new service industries and manufacturing. Food, clothing, mining, hardware, and all kinds of luxuries were needed in California. When mining methods changed from panning to excavation, heavy machinery was needed. In under one decade, the Northern Californians started their own iron industry. They manufactured steam engines, hydraulic pumps, and stamp mills. By 1861, more than one thousand people worked in the production of mining equipment in San Francisco alone. Powder works were opened in California as early as 1855, completely replacing the imported explosives the people had relied upon.

Gold mining demanded other industries as well. Lumber was needed, not only for house building but also for the support beams of mines. Just one decade after the beginning of the California Gold Rush, Humboldt and Mendocino Counties were producing over thirty-five million board feet per year. As for food, California was quick to establish flour mills. It had none when the Gold Rush began back in 1848, but by the 1860s, two hundred mills were in operation. California produced enough flour to feed its people and export it to Japan, China, and parts of Europe. Due to the rapid increase of people, the clothing industry bloomed. Most notable are the Mission Woolen Mills, which became the largest producers of cloth in the West, and Levi Strauss, who, together with Jacob Davis, invented the fashionable blue jeans. At first, these riveted pants were made for miners since they were sturdy enough to endure the hard working conditions. Over the centuries, they became a fashion staple across the world. Farming was another industry that bloomed. Many miners who weren't successful in finding gold turned to growing fruit and vegetables or running dairy farms. They produced enough food to cover the whole Pacific Coast region.

But the Gold Rush wasn't only a local economic event. The products made in California were exported around the world. During the California Gold Rush, in 1853, Commodore Matthew Perry opened the Japanese ports to trade with the United States. California, being in the West, benefited greatly from the newly established contacts. In general, California's farm products were highly valued in Asia, and San Francisco merchants enjoyed great success in trade with China and Japan.

The influence of the California Gold Rush on Europe was less significant, but it could still be felt. Norway, whose economy completely depended on transportation, trade, and commerce, was probably influenced the most by the economic growth of California and the US. It recognized the possibilities in the newly emerging economy of the Pacific Coast and stressed the importance of building a canal across the Isthmus of Panama. The iron manufacturers of Norway also saw the potential new market in California for railways and railroad equipment. France was also influenced by the Gold Rush on a deeper level. Thousands of people saw the opportunity to settle and start their own businesses in California. Many young people gave up on the revolution that raged in France in 1848 and went to search for new job opportunities in the US. But once Napoleon III established political stability in France in 1852, the immigration to America ebbed. One million Germans emigrated to the US during the Gold Rush, and 300,000 of them settled in California. Many Germans established themselves as farmers and/or started grocery businesses. And when it came to Great Britain, around fifty thousand skilled miners came to California during the 1850s. More than 500,000 British immigrants followed. During the early years of the Gold Rush, British stock companies invested over ten million dollars in California's mining companies. They didn't earn much, but they established their presence in California, which allowed them to expand their interests. Soon, the stock companies of Great Britain started investing in California's developing industries, and they helped propel the local iron and food production.

The influx of California's gold into the world markets created price spikes in Europe. The costs of goods increased all over the world, but it was most significantly felt in California itself, as well as in Great Britain. However, the influx of people in California demanded increased imports, and Great Britain was ready to fulfill those demands. Between 1850 and 1855, British exports to California numbered around $2 million per year. These booming exports brought new prosperity to the British Isles, and the economic stability brought increased demands for workers and the rise of wages. So, even though the prices were rising, most people had no trouble earning the necessary money to survive.

In the Pacific Rim countries, the California Gold Rush caused a shortage of workers. Many Hawaiian sugar plantation workers left for California, hoping to find employment in the goldfields. A similar thing happened in China, where people decided to leave for either California or Hawaii (where they sought to fill the empty sugar plantations). However, it should be noted that the Gold Rush coincided with the Taiping Rebellion, a civil war that caused famine and the loss of properties in China. Thus, it is no wonder so many people had to leave their home country and seek fortune elsewhere.

Due to the hype of the California Gold Rush, people tried to find precious metals in South Africa and Australia, and they were successful, further adding to the influx of gold to the world's economy.

Conclusion

January 24th, 1848, is the approximate date given to the discovery of gold in California. James Wilson Marshall, the man who first found gold near Sutter's Mill, was never certain what date he found that first nugget. Later in life, he said he thought it was January 19th, but several other accounts contradict Marshall's claim. Some historians even believe it wasn't Marshall who found the gold in the first place but an unknown Native American mill worker. This Native American is remembered as "Indian Jim," and according to the story, he gave the gold nugget, which was the size of a brass button, to a white mill worker who later showed it to Marshall. The problem here is not that we don't know how it exactly happened but the lack of evidence itself. There were only a few witnesses to the discovery of gold and even fewer records about it. Everyone who was involved in finding that first gold nugget was a commoner, an uneducated person with little to no incentive to describe the events in the written word.

Even though the California Gold Rush is not an event that is commemorated in the US, it is certainly an event that shaped the country. The massive influx of immigrants into the US, as well as the influx of California's gold into the economy, defined the world's history of the period. Previously sparsely populated regions now had to organize a state and become part of the US. To keep in touch with the families these immigrants had left behind, the United States had to invest in the development of communication, infrastructure, and transportation. The distance between California and the rest of the US had to be bridged. But it was the people who came to California that started the state's production industry, agriculture, and the many small and large businesses.

The importance of the discovery of gold on the development of California is still seen in its modern symbols. The state's motto is "Eureka," an ancient Greek word that means "I have found it." The state is still nicknamed the Golden State, but it no longer symbolizes only the Gold Rush. Instead, this nickname today means that California is a place of prosperity, new beginnings, and hope. Route 49, which runs through the Sierra Nevada foothills, is aptly named after the forty-niners, a brave generation that pioneered the Gold Rush. Also, the sign of Route 49 is shaped like a miner's spade to commemorate all those people who ventured to California in search of gold.

Part 3: 1906 San Francisco Earthquake

A Captivating Guide to the Deadliest Earthquake in the History of the United States

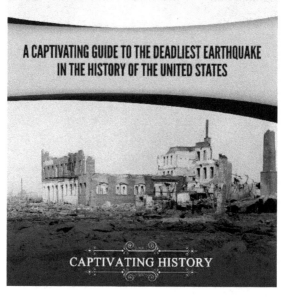

Introduction

When we think of the solid earth under our feet, it gives us a sense of security and stability. But what happens when that seeming stability suddenly heaves up and literally shakes the foundations of a whole city and every living thing in it?

Earthquakes are not a new phenomenon, and many people have survived seismic events of varying intensity. But those who felt the intensity of the 1906 earthquake in San Francisco and its tragic aftermath experienced a catastrophe to which few, if any in history, could relate.

By the early 1900s, San Francisco had gone through decades of transformation, turning itself into a bustling city known as the "gateway to the Pacific." Between its busy coastal ports, thriving entertainment scene, and a strengthening military presence, San Francisco had gained a reputation as an important hub in the western United States. But as we are all too aware, disasters, especially those of the natural variety, strike indiscriminately, caring little for what humans consider valuable—including their lives and those of their families.

Though the city itself was damaged—buildings fell and burned, streets heaved and cracked—it's those within the city whose stories we find the most compelling. That earthquake in 1906 shook a city to its foundations, but it also shook the lives of real people, some of whom did not survive the initial quake or the fires that followed.

We'll walk through not only the facts and timeline of this historic earthquake but allow those that were there to continue to "tell" their stories. Eyewitness accounts have painted a picture of seemingly unstoppable catastrophes piled on top of one another, split-second decisions that saved lives, other decisions that led to further disaster, and the helplessness of many to control the fate of themselves or the city. We'll recount stories of heroism alongside heartbreak, the dangers that followed the initial quake and aftershocks, the relief response from those who came to help, and how San Francisco started to rebuild itself from the ashes of a disaster.

As you read the accounts of what happened, imagine yourself in the picture as the quake happened. Would you have been on a ship at sea, on the commuter train, working on your farm, or violently shaken from your bed the moment the quake occurred? Would you have thought quickly on your feet to escape, run to save others, or prayed out of fear? They are questions that are hard to answer.

Chapter 1 – The Earth Shifts

On April 18th, 1906, the early morning streets of San Francisco were quiet, as they were on most days. The noise and fanfare of the previous night's opera and vaudeville shows had died down, with theatergoers long gone home, waiting to soon wake to the new day. Though everything was still on the surface, out to sea, about ten miles deep within the earth, the San Andreas Fault was about to slip.

One hundred and fifty miles from San Francisco, the crew of the schooner *John A. Campbell* were asleep in their bunks as their ship cut its way through the Pacific Ocean. Without a moment's notice, below the ocean bed, an incredible energy was unleashed—a force that exceeded all the explosive power used during World War II. As the schooner rose and crashed back down into the sea, the alarmed crew were jolted from their beds. Understandably thinking the boat had rammed into a shipwreck or perhaps a whale, they hastened to the deck. But when the puzzled captain and crew looked over the rails, there was nothing to be seen.

The shockwave, moving through the sea at two miles per second, did not take long to reach the steamer ship *Argo*, which was easily cruising through the calm sea. The shockwave shot through the water forty fathoms below, causing the ship to shudder suddenly and severely. Like the crew of the *John A. Campbell*, those aboard the *Argo* were caught completely off guard and assumed that their ship had struck something like a reef or a raft of floating logs. The jolt buckled the sturdy ship's steel plates, and bolts were forcefully blown out of their riveting. For one horrifying moment, her captain believed that his whole ship was breaking apart. Like the schooner's baffled crew, when the *Argo*'s men checked the sea, there was nothing in sight but ocean. By the time they looked out into the open expanse, the earthquake was already reaching land.

Near the shore, the tide gauge registered a rather small tsunami wave measuring about three inches in height. An extraordinarily unimpressive blip, it gave no indication of the force that was about to be unleashed onto the shore.

At seven thousand miles per hour, the power unleashed by the earthquake blasted into the California shoreline, frighteningly close to the Point Arena lighthouse.[1] The force caused the structure, which stood 110 feet tall, to sway frantically on its base. Though it had withstood decades of ferocious weather, the lantern of the lighthouse beacon easily cracked and shattered, raining a shimmer of glass down to its floor.

As the incredible force continued south, animals in the region sensed the coming shift right before it hit, becoming restless and agitated. Horses kicked about in their corrals. A milk cart rattled loudly as the milkman tried to calm his excited horse.

The human population near San Francisco, though, had no inkling of what was coming. Brigadier General Frederick Funston, the commander of the Presidio military outpost at the time, said that before the quake, there was "not a single sound" of warning— "no shrieking of whistles, no clanging of bells."

---

[1] The Point Arena lighthouse is ninety miles north of San Francisco.

But it was within the city where some of the most dramatic scenes unfolded and damages were felt.

Chapter 2 – A City Shakes

At 5:12 a.m., a significant foreshock jolted the ground underneath the city of San Francisco. If this was not enough to grab the attention of those within the city, what was about to come shook everyone and everything to their very foundations. About twenty to twenty-five seconds after the initial shock, the full force of the quake rolled through the ground and was felt in all its 8.0 magnitude of intensity.[2] The energy released underneath was terrifying in its power.

Both those sleeping and awake were thrown into an immediate panic, and anyone who was able to gain their footing stumbled about, terrified. Their floors heaved, and the walls around them shook, and the people instinctively sought safety, with many running into the street in various states of dress, leaving their valuables behind.

In recounting how it sounded and felt, John Farish, a mining engineer staying at the St. Francis Hotel, said that he woke up to a loud rumbling. He compared it to "a strong wind rushing through a forest mixed with waves breaking against a cliff." Farish referred to

---

[2] Though the earthquake is generally said to have been an 8.0 on the seismological Richter scale, various sources value it from as low as 7.7 to as high as 8.3 on the Richter scale.

the main quake as a "concussion" type explosion, like that of "a huge blast" that "shook the building to its foundations."

As frightened people poured into the street, screams of terror rose up around the city. Others fell into feverish prayer, fearing that a divine judgment had fallen upon the city. With the church bells shaking and clanging in a violent cacophony, no one could blame a soul for thinking that the end had come. The furious ringing created an ominous soundtrack, a chaotic backdrop as chimneys toppled onto their houses and through roofs, crushing some as they still lay in their beds. Towers crashed down from their heights, and entire walls crumbled into the streets. This violent shock lasted for about a minute—a minute that must have felt unending to those experiencing it.

Simple wood-frame houses were no match for the violent quaking, their timbers splintering and the structures they held collapsing into rubble. Large gas reservoirs and sprawling factory buildings did not fare much better. This was exemplified over at the city's gas and electric company buildings, where a tall smokestack at one of the stations toppled, killing a man in the company's yard. Warehouse walls cracked and bulged, threatening to snap. Buildings that stayed upright shifted from their foundation by two or three feet.

The streets themselves heaved up and split apart as if with gaping wounds. Future police commissioner Jesse Cook heard what he described as a "deep and terrible" rumble. As he turned to look down the street, he watched in horror as the street rose up and undulated, rolling toward him like ocean waves.

Produce dealers, with their wagons on the streets, were thrown about as the ground heaved. Some carts toppled over, still hitched to their horses, with drivers and animals lying dead in the streets.

Underground, gas and water mains ruptured, releasing deadly gas and floods of water into the streets. Telegraph poles rocked back and forth, creating a tangle of sparking wires that lay twisted together along with electrical lines.

The unusual rotary motion of the quake caused seemingly unbendable structures like steel streetcar rails, underground pipelines, bridges, and others to become unimaginably twisted and mangled. Metal squealed and ground out of its original shapes. The twelve-story Call building, a steel skyscraper, shifted off its base by two feet, its insides twisted by the force.

Over at the Bush Street fire station, San Francisco Fire Chief Dennis Sullivan was asleep in his third-floor residence. When the quake struck, he leaped to his feet and ran toward his wife in the adjoining room. At the same moment, the smokestacks high atop the neighboring California Hotel collapsed, sending a mass of brick and mortar crashing through the station roof. The wave of heavy debris carried Chief Sullivan and his wife with it right through to the first floor, mortally wounding the chief. Unfortunately, Sullivan did not recover from the severe chest and head injuries sustained in the collapse and tragically died three days later. It was a loss that was to be more deeply felt in the coming days.

Chaotic scenes like this quickly unfolded across the entire city and just outside of it, which was where the San Francisco commuter train was making its way to the city. The two jolts caused the engine car to jackknife along with four other cars. The rest of the train swayed back and forth wildly, forcing wheels to come off and toppling its cars onto their sides. Dairy farmers milking their cattle were thrown to the ground as the frightened animals stampeded, with the cows becoming so traumatized that they couldn't give milk for days.

Though the biggest shock went on for about a minute, relatively smaller shocks, some as big as 6.4 on the Richter scale, continued to rock the city until noon. The severity of the initial quakes and the smaller shocks that followed was enough to destroy the center of the city. It is unclear how many died that morning, but the earthquake proved to be just the beginning, and unbelievably, it was the less destructive part of the disaster.

Chapter 3 – Infernos Consume

It wasn't long before columns of smoke began to appear around the city. In the business district, four separate fires reared up around the mostly brick buildings, some of which were considered to be "fireproof."

General Frederick Funston wasted no time springing into action, rushing toward the fires burning on Sansome and California Streets. It was not even 6 a.m., and the crisis looming from the fire was already evident. The city's firemen, who were without a chief, were still on the scene by the time the general arrived, but they had another crisis to contend with—a lack of water. Water main breaks caused by the earthquake compounded the problem of an already inadequate water system.

General Funston immediately saw that the firemen, as well as the police, would need the help of troops at nearby outposts. With no other way of getting a message to his men, he "wildly dashed about" as he tried to flag down passing motorists, all of whom ignored his desperate gesticulating. He was forced to run to the nearest army stables and send messages around the city for all available men to report to Police Chief Jeremiah Dinan at the Hall of Justice.

By the time 9 a.m. came around, citizens, as well as authorities, began to see the stark reality that the city was burning. Hundreds of fires were rapidly springing up around the city, even claiming some of the strongest buildings that had initially withstood the earthquake. The fires surrounded and attacked everything, including the tallest skyscrapers in the city.

Flames shot out wildly from the windows of large hotels and smaller lodging houses alike, triumphantly claiming them all and leaving only charred walls as a reminder of what once stood there. As flames marched toward the Palace Hotel, a longtime favorite of those visiting the city, guests quickly fled and with little time to spare. Curls of fire soon reached the building and turned it into an inferno before moving on to its neighboring structures.

Unsurprisingly, the area of the city that housed its newspaper offices also quickly came under threat. Though the Examiner Building had collapsed in the earthquake, the sturdier Chronicle Building remained standing. But full of papery ammunition, the buildings became tinderboxes, unable to withstand the fiery assault.

Many watched helplessly as landmark after landmark was claimed by the flames. The Grand Opera, the Emporium, St. Ignatius Church, the Bohemian Club, and many others represented tremendous losses to San Francisco's financial, art, and religious communities.

Even more distressing than seeing important city buildings disappear was watching their own residences burn. The fire claimed mansions and humble wooden structures alike.

Since the fires had moved swiftly from house to house and neighborhood to neighborhood, many had no time to save any of their belongings and were in the street with little more than the clothes on their backs. Some who were able to grab their valuables threw them in ditches or covered holes to try to protect them from the flames, setting up crude markers in order to find and retrieve their things after the fire had passed. Others tried to move their things to safer locations, dragging overloaded trunks through the streets with ropes and carrying blankets, boxes, and even pets in their arms as they tried to rush away, unsure as to where they would go. Those who could find a wagon to hire to take their belongings would have paid exorbitant prices for the luxury.

Not all buildings were lost, however. The heroic persistence of firefighters and citizens saved many structures. Maybe the most remarkable example of this was the United States Mint, which housed millions of dollars in gold and silver.

Frank Leach, the superintendent, along with several other male employees, raced to the Mint following the initial quake. Men were stationed on every floor of the building, including the basement and roof. Using the Mint's fire apparatus and hoses, employees and firemen took turns laboriously hand pumping water from the basement.

The victory over the fire was far from sure, though. The fires were reducing the surrounding buildings to charcoal and looked to claim the Mint next. Flames licked at the windows and pushed their way through the rear of the building, forcing the people to temporarily retreat. The workers found their ground and fought back. For seven grueling hours, they fought, hosing down windows and the roof and swiftly putting out smaller fires that sprang up, keeping them from growing into monstrous infernos. In the end, the quick thinking of the employees and the tireless efforts of all on the scene managed to score a victory for the building. Though it did not remain unscathed, the damage was minor, especially compared to the surrounding neighborhood.

Elsewhere, police officers and detectives employed bravery and resourcefulness to save what they could from the Hall of Justice. There came a point in the morning where it was obvious to the men that the Hall could not be saved from the fire. But that didn't mean they wouldn't try to save all the important police records contained within. A detail of officers was assigned to quickly move the files to

Portsmouth Square. They covered the records with a canvas, hoping to protect it from ash and other elements, and kept vigil over the collection. Supplied with ample courage and other provisions, they still lacked access to the one thing that they needed the most—water.

The fire rapidly moved toward the square, surrounding it and keeping the officers trapped in the area. Fiery cinders rained down on the canvas covering the records, and the men fought through the intense heat to beat down the fires that ignited. It was only a temporary band-aid, though. Without water, the records would be lost. Desperate to find something they could use to quench the flames, officers ran into a nearby bar, grabbing all the bottles of beer they could find. For twenty-four hours, they doused the canvas with beer, dampening the embers that fell, and in the end, they managed to save the valuable records for which they had fought so hard.

The officers at Plymouth Square were not the only ones to use everything at their disposal to save what was important to them. Directly following the quake, some in the city had the forethought to fill up their bathtub with buckets of water, likely relieved that they were later able to use those reserves to squelch the fires that threatened their homes. Others without water reserves used wine and vinegar to save their residences, dousing flames that tried to take their humble houses.

At some point, every fire company in the city faced the same devastating problem—broken water mains and lack of water sources typically used to fight fires. Like others in similar situations around the city, it didn't stop them from using ingenuity and resourcefulness to continue the fight.

When the water mains broke, all that water went somewhere, with tens of thousands of gallons ponding in the sewers. Firemen dropped hoses into every pool of water they could reach, eventually draining their sources. Firemen also tapped into the city's 23 water cisterns, which gave them up to possibly 100,000 gallons to use in the fight.

Another saving grace for the city was the fact that a portion of it sat on or near the waterfront. Firemen dropped hoses into the bay and were able to save many buildings in the area due to its endless water supply. Yet, this, too, had its limits. Eventually, fires burned outside the reach of the bay water hoses, and firemen were forced to find other solutions.

The bravery and tenacity of those who fought the fires are well documented, and many fought until they collapsed and could give no more. Water, wine, vinegar, beer, and other liquids all played a part in saving the city from complete devastation, but the firemen realized that it still wouldn't be enough. They needed to use one more resource at their disposal—dynamite.

Chapter 4 – The Dynamite Solution

Fear began to mount that the conflagrations around the city might not be able to be controlled. Disaster loomed. Fighting the fires would test the best of the city's firemen with a job that seemed all but hopeless. City authorities finally concluded that the only hope for taming the fires would come from using dynamite.

Much like controlled fire breaks created by wildfire fighters today, San Francisco authorities believed that they could halt the progress of the fires by taking away the source of fuel. Troops and firemen would get ahead of the flames and blow up buildings in the fire's path, leaving little for the fire to consume and interrupting the path of travel.

General Frederick Funston wasted no time organizing this endeavor. He mobilized troops, firefighters, and police officers alike, sending them out around the city to strategically create the fire breaks. Their plan was quickly put into effect, and it wasn't long before thunderous explosions were being heard around the city.

The men did not go into this planning to demolish every building near a fire. They proceeded carefully at first, blowing up one or two buildings at a time, hoping to keep the damage to a minimum. Such caution proved to be ineffective against the determined and swiftly moving infernos. The men upped their measures and took down half of a block at a time, but this, too, was proving to be too little. Flames continued to leap over rubble and through the newly made gaps between buildings. Dynamite squads had no choice but to take dynamite to whole city blocks, taking a scorched-earth approach and leveling everything. Everything the explosives touched was blown to dust.

As dangerous as it was to fight the fires that raged around the city, being part of an explosives team was exponentially more so. This is illustrated by the story of Lieutenant Charles Pulis, the commander of one of the city's Light Artillery companies.

In charge of dynamiting the Sixth and Jesse street blocks, he and Police Captain Henry Gleeson laid the heavy charges inside of a building. According to police records from the time, Pulis lit the fuse, and both men fled toward the door. They wouldn't make it out on time. Unable to beat the swiftly burning fuse, the explosion blew the men out of the building and into the street. Wreckage from the blast rained down on their unconscious forms. Pulis's injuries were severe. Besides a fractured skull, he broke several other bones and sustained internal injuries. Though it was a near-fatal incident, both men survived.

Amid incidents like that of Lieutenant Pulis and Captain Gleeson, it was obvious that dynamite in the hands of the untrained was not only extremely dangerous but also did not prove to be as effective as they hoped. In some cases, it caused more harm than good. Yet, with the life of the city on the line, this was too important to be left to volunteers ignorant in the proper use of these explosives. It was time to bring in the experts.

Three skilled explosives engineers, the best and most trusted, were selected from the Mare Island Naval Shipyard by Admiral Bowman McCalla. With Captain McBride in charge of two gunners, the trio made up the city's new ace dynamite squad.

The men were ordered to stop the flames without regard to the cost of property damage. With the flames continuing to spread, there was no other choice—it was the only way to salvage the doomed city. But if they were going to stop an out-of-control conflagration, they would need the firepower to match it.

With the agreement of city authorities, the trio decided to make their stand on Van Ness Avenue. Fires from the burning business district quickly made their way toward them. Though none of the buildings in that area had yet been touched by flames or embers, they couldn't be allowed to remain standing. There was no time to waste if the trio wanted to cut it off. Systematically, they set their charges. Terrifying, powerful thunder reverberated through the area as the explosives took down one block after another. Not a building remained standing.

When the dynamite and guncotton were done with their work, a million dollars in debris and dust formed a gaping firebreak. The fire made its approach and reached its tentacles out to the ruins. It can only be imaged how everyone present held their collective breaths as the flames reached the debris field. Though there was some fuel for the fire among the wreckage, it was not enough to feed the hungry flames for long. Water pumped from the bay helped complete the mission. The fires that once raged wild soon burned what little they could and then died amid what remained of the neighborhood.

Though the dynamite did its share in stopping the fires near Van Ness Avenue, the real credit went to the dynamite squad trio. Their skillful and courageous efforts were what halted the main conflagration, and their heroic efforts are credited with saving the city from total fiery destruction. Though they made history, once their work was done, the three men quietly departed, leaving the weary firemen to watch over the smoldering ruins.

Chapter 5 – Eyewitnesses Tell Their Stories

While firemen, police officers, and soldiers quickly mobilized around the city and gave reports of what they did and saw, many ordinary citizens had harrowing tales of their own. Some, like those in the following accounts, were struck with terror as they were shaken from their beds. What they described were near apocalyptic scenes. Here are some of their stories.

Businessman **Jerome Clark** started his story from a vantage point outside the city proper. As he lived across the San Francisco Bay, he only felt minor quakes at home early that morning. Unaware of what was happening on the other side of the bay, he took his usual commuter ferry to the city. As he stepped off the ferry, he was met with a cataclysmic scene. He described flames seething in every direction that he looked.

As he stood gazing, slowly taking in the scene, a nearby five-story building succumbed to the flames and came crashing down. The downward force of the crash acted as a fan, sweeping flames across Market Street, where they laid claim to one of the new "fireproof" buildings. As he turned his attention to the street itself, he saw that the earthquake had caused it to sink three or four feet in some areas while rising in cracked, mishappen humps four or five feet high in other areas.

G. A. Raymond was a guest at the Palace Hotel, and he was still asleep when the earthquake struck. As he woke up, he was thrown out of his bed by the massive jolt. Trying to find his footing, he fell as the floor shook violently. Leaving the $600 in gold he had stashed under his pillow, he grabbed his clothing and ran to the lobby. Suddenly, the lights went out, and he rushed to the door along with others.

Once outside, he witnessed "a sight that he never wanted to see again." He looked up into the dawning light to see an ominous sight—a sky raining stones. They fell all around him, crushing many to death. Huge buildings swayed like grass in the breeze, and a sound that he described as "100 cannons going off at one time" filled the air. Fire shot out from various buildings.

Unsure what was happening, he asked the man next to him. Before the man could even get the words out, "a thousand bricks fell" on the man, killing him before Raymond's eyes. Raymond fled in a panic, with people all around him crying, calling for help, and even praying, thinking it was the actual end of the world.

As he ran, he met a Catholic priest who urged Raymond to follow him to the ferry. They rushed down the street, witnessing young and old being crushed under falling debris while others crawled out from under already fallen debris.

Streets cracked and opened into gaping chasms. A frightened drove of cattle rushed past Raymond and disappeared. Moving closer to where he last saw them, he peered over the edge of one of the chasms. He could see that they had indeed fallen and been swallowed into the abyss-like fissures. These sights made him "crazy with fear."

John Barrett, who, at the time, was the news editor for the *San Francisco Examiner*, tells a similar story of the scene that unfolded during the quake. He described the initial seconds of the quake as feeling like the "earth slipping gently from under his feet," causing him to stagger and reel. As the quake intensified, the "sickening swaying" caused him to fall in the street, unable to regain his footing. He later described it as feeling unable to move, as if suctioned to the earth by a huge vacuum. All around him, people were on all fours "like crawling bugs."

As buildings crumbled around him, Barrett felt as though his "head was split with the roar that crashed" in his ears. He saw an ironworker on his way to the Union Iron Works. A cornice from the building he stood near toppled down, crushing the unfortunate man with his dinner pail still in hand.

Though it seemed near an eternity, the main quake soon ended. As Barrett tried to return to his feet, the aftershocks that immediately followed continued to send him reeling. Once the shaking stopped, he could see the damage through the dust clouds darkening the sky.

Everything around him lay twisted and mangled, the streets gaping wide open. He could smell gas from the broken main. Then rose "a horrible chorus of human cries of agony" as families lay buried in the rubble of their homes and fires began to burn around the city.

Barrett returned to his feet, looked at his colleagues, and proclaimed, "This is going to be a hell of a day." Little did he know how prophetic those words would turn out to be. Describing the hellish scene playing out around the city, he later recalled it as one of "agony, death, and a flaming torch," as if "some fire demon" rushed around, setting everything ablaze. The fire shot up everywhere, yet the flaming destruction was just beginning.

Chapter 6 – Tales of Heroism and Heartbreak

Though heroic by their very nature, firemen, soldiers, sailors, and police officers were not the only ones to show courage and strength during this emergency. Ordinary citizens, at times working alongside professionals, showed incredible bravery and compassion toward others.

Many were rescued from crumbled buildings and unstoppable fires, but there were also many heartbreaking instances of those who could not be saved in time. The following accounts illustrate the many scenes that occurred across the city.

On Folsom Street, one man was fortunate enough to be saved from the wreckage of a lodging house. Two other men inside did not fare as well. Before he got out, he heard their conversation:

"I'm not hurt, but there's a beam across my back, and I can't get out from under it."

The second man responded, "I'm caught too; it's my wrist. Don't worry; they'll get us out."

The heartrending optimism of the men is hard to read about since before rescuers could dig them from where they were trapped, the fires came and forced the rescuers to retreat. Helplessly, rescuers watched as the fire leaped into the wreckage, claiming everything and everyone inside.

Some heroic deeds required exceptional strength and courage to carry out as they came at a high cost. Eyewitness Max Fast watched as the Windsor Hotel caught fire. Three men went to the roof to get away from the inferno inside, but once there, they were trapped with no way down. Seeing their panic and understanding the terrible fiery fate that awaited them, a military officer on the scene had a hard decision to make. Wanting to save them from further agony, he felt giving them a painless death was the kinder option. And so, he ordered his men to shoot them as five thousand people looked on.

Those officers were not the only ones that had to make a painful decision like this. Eyewitness Adolphus Busch also described a chilling scene, which he said was the most terrible thing he ever saw. Policemen and citizens worked urgently to rescue a man who was pinned by the wreckage of a building. The trapped man watched in silent terror as the flames crept closer, eventually reaching his feet. As the fire began to burn him, the man begged the police officer to kill him, saving him from an even worse fate. After taking down the man's name and address, the officer pulled out his gun and, squeezing the trigger, shot the man in the head, killing him and instantly ending his suffering.

At the bottom of the Russian Hill area, an affluent neighborhood, stood small frame houses occupied by immigrants. Without bias or reservation, an army corps volunteer moved quickly to try to outrun the fire and warned people of the flames swiftly coming toward them and their humble homes. The flames were too fast, however. Before they could get out of an old frame house, three women became trapped on the top floor. The building was a virtual tinderbox waiting to ignite. Thinking quickly on his feet, a man tore up a piece of fencing and used it to climb to the window where the distressed women huddled. He managed to grab two of the women and slid them down the rail. They reached the ground, injured but safe. The fire reached the roof and spread quickly. The man struggled to quickly save the last woman, but as he did, both fell into the flames and were consumed.

Accounts like these occurred all over the city. Sailors formed firefighting task forces and leaped into action. Firemen battled for thirty-six hours, strained under the weight of conditions they had never even imagined facing, let alone having experienced before.

It's not possible to contain all the stories of heroism and heartrending loss in one place. Firemen, in particular, worked tirelessly and selflessly to save the city and their fellow citizens, knowing their own homes had been destroyed and going without sleep, with little food or water, and without even knowing what happened to their own families.

However, it wasn't just fire that threatened the city. There was also a difficult and thankless task that fell to the patrolling sentries—protecting the city from crime.

Chapter 7 – Crime Curbed Through Violence

"As it has come to my attention that thieves are taking advantage of the present deplorable conditions and are plying their nefarious vocations among the ruins in our city, all peace officers are ordered to instantly kill anyone caught looting or committing any other serious crimes."

—*E. E. Schmitz, Mayor*

Not all in the city showed a heroic nature during this time of crisis. Criminals took advantage of the chaos to loot and commit other crimes. Authorities were certainly aware that unsavory opportunists would engage in criminal activities, and so, they swiftly moved into action. Within mere hours of the quake, San Francisco Mayor Eugene Schmitz drafted and posted a proclamation that could give additional temptation to looters. He directed that gas and electricity be turned off indefinitely, plunging the city into total darkness at night.

Though the proclamation also instituted a citywide curfew that commanded people to stay home from dark until daylight, the mayor knew the order would not be obeyed by all. Knowing that looters would find the darkness of night to be far too tempting, the mayor gave them a reason to take pause. In a declaration that many found shocking, the proclamation ordered federal troops, city police officers, and special officers to "kill any and all persons" found not just looting but also committing any other crime.

This warning was no mere idle threat. In a stark demonstration of what happened to those who dared defy the law, the body of a man shot by authorities was thrown atop a pile of bricks and stones, the bullet hole in his chest visible to all. Pinned to his chest was a chilling sign that sternly cautioned, "Take warning!"

Others also reported seeing dead bodies left lying in the streets where they fell, each with a placard that read "shot for stealing" or "Looter." It was obvious that crime would not be tolerated and that justice would be swiftly and summarily executed on the spot.

The stiff penalty for crime aside, citizens now believed that the proclamation was also a declaration to suspend constitutional law and institute martial law throughout the city. Most did not realize that the mayor had neither actually declared martial law nor had the power to do so, and those that did have the power (the governor and President Theodore Roosevelt) had not declared it. However, the city was too busy fighting the rising crisis to protest a move that many would later declare unconstitutional or even dictatorial.

Though it may have created some confusion among authorities as to who actually had control of the city, most citizens felt reassured by the heavy police and military presence. However, not everyone took comfort from that. Journalist Henry Anderson Lafler lamented the atmosphere that descended upon the city that had been brought on by the presence of so many soldiers. He likened the atmosphere to a medieval siege—a "city captured in war." Later, he bemoaned the situation, saying that the people had "been suddenly gripped by the throat by a stupid soldiery and held fast" while the city burned. For others, the morning bugle calls, the pacing sentry patrols, and the officers on horseback only added to the perception that the city was under military occupation.

Yet, the widespread perception that the authorities had the city under control could not be underestimated in its effectiveness. The sight of soldiers with bayoneted guns marching through the streets was an unspoken signal to citizens that order would be kept.

Despite the explicit warnings and the presence of one thousand patrolmen from various branches of the police and military, some unscrupulous individuals remained undeterred.[3] One of the most unsettling and unspeakable crimes occurring around the city was the robbing of the dead—a crime seemingly easy to get away with in the middle of a burning city. Witnesses recounted stories of those who found out how strictly the law was enforced and how "justice" was meted out without mercy. Soldiers did not hesitate to "shoot down the ghouls" who dared desecrate the dead.

This is illustrated in the story of one citizen who witnessed a man trying to cut the stiffened fingers off a dead woman in an attempt to steal her rings. Three soldiers saw what he was doing and, chasing the man, ordered him to put his hands in the air. Instead, the would-be robber drew his gun. The soldiers, backed up by six policemen, immediately raised their rifles and fired, hitting the man with nine bullets. His body was then unceremoniously taken to an alley and disposed of on the cement.

In a separate incident, a thief found a young woman who had fainted, lying unconscious on the floor of a hotel. Instead of trying to simply take the rings off her fingers, the brute cut off her finger and ran, leaving her helpless to the ravages of the nearing fire. Though he escaped any well-deserved justice, it demonstrated the "ghoulish" nature that some allowed themselves to fall into.

---

[3] Though criminal acts still took place, the heavy patrol presence did have a positive effect. Many citizens were documented noting that crime, especially the robbing of the dead, would have been "many more times prevalent were it not for the constant vigilance on all sides, as well as the summary justice."

These would not be isolated happenings. A group of fourteen men found the empty US Mint building too enticing of an opportunity to pass up. They hatched a plot and brazenly attempted to break into and steal the unattended money, counting on authorities being distracted elsewhere. They underestimated the vigilance of those on duty, though. During the attempt, they were shot down by a guard after refusing to comply with his command to cease and desist.

Eyewitnesses recounted many stories of thieves being shot or, even more gruesomely, run through with bayonets while in the act of stealing. For instance, a sailor patrolling Market Street saw a man digging through the ruins of a jewelry shop, apparently intent on stealing what he found. Upon seeing him, the sailor shot at the man three times, but the man somehow remained untouched and ran. The sailor chased after him and ran the man through with his bayonet, bringing him to the ground.

Not all such enforcements of the mayor's proclamation happened in the moment. Three thieves who were caught in three separate crimes were taken before a crowd of ten thousand people, where they were lined up and shot. It made the seriousness of the order hard to deny.

Some soldiers had an excessively strict interpretation of the law against stealing and looting. They also extended this to those who tried to take advantage of the situation by price gouging. This was evidenced in the case of a beer delivery man who agreed to transport a family and their belongings. When they got to their destination, the driver demanded that he be paid twenty-five dollars, which was much higher than the normal rate. The man who hitched a ride was down to his last five dollars and offered it to the driver, but the driver refused to unload the family's belongings unless he was paid the sum he demanded. Soldiers witnessed the exchange and demanded that the driver accept the five dollars and give the family their things. When the driver refused the order, the soldiers held up a watch and gave the driver three minutes to comply. After the three minutes expired, the driver still refused to budge on the price, and the soldiers ran him through with their bayonets.

But deadly clashes were not just taking place between citizens and authorities; tension ran high between those keeping order as well. One such clash was reported by an eyewitness named Mr. Fast, who saw the encounter go down in Jefferson Square. There, a policeman and soldier argued over who should pick up a dead body and put it in the wagon. Both men ordered the other to do so, and when each refused, the exchange became heated. Finally, the soldier pulled out his gun and shot the policeman dead, right in the street.

The tension felt by the patrolmen tasked with defending the city from crime also led to some even more unfortunate stories of those being shot due to woeful misunderstandings. In one instance, a man who owned a grocery store saw that the fire was rapidly approaching and that his business would not be spared. So, he opened the doors and allowed anyone in the area to take what they wanted. This information was not known to a passing soldier, who, after seeing a man walk out of the store with groceries in his arms, assumed he was stealing. Without a word, he ran up to the innocent man and stabbed him with his bayonet.

A bank clerk, who was ordered to search the ruins of his bank, was mistaken for a looter and shot. There were also numerous regrettable stories of people being mistaken for looters and shot while going into their own homes.

Others were shot for the most minor of infractions, such as washing their hands in drinking water that was intended to ease the thirst of those gathered in a park. Two men tried to get around the mayor's order of keeping the city in darkness during the night and lit candles; soldiers shot them down through the windows of their respective homes. A woman who lit a fire on her cook stove was no also exception, for she too was shot.

Though children caught stealing were spared immediate death, they were not immune from the law or punishment for breaking it. Justice in those instances was meted out with a beating, after which the child was forced to wear a humiliating sign in public announcing "I am a thief."

Soldiers were not the only ones who executed the mayor's orders regarding looters. Some criminals fell by vigilante justice, doled out by citizens who would not stand idly by. One major example of this was performed by a group of miners near the Palace Hotel. When they found a man trying to rob a corpse, they took immediate action. Without waiting for any sort of authority figure, they took hold of the thief, found a rope, and promptly strung him up from a standing beam in the hotel ruins. Just moments later, the crowd caught a fellow criminal and quickly strung him up next to the first thief. The pair dangled together in the doorway, making for a grisly scene.

Baseless shootings also occurred when ordinary citizens took matters into their own hands. The final straw came when a citizens' patrol mistakenly shot Major H. C. Tilden and two others in his vehicle. The major, a prominent member of the General Relief Committee, was in a car that was being used as an ambulance, but the shooters claimed that they failed to see the Red Cross banner hung on the side. They also justified the shooting by saying that the vehicle hadn't stopped when they challenged it, but they also gave no lawful reason for having made the attempt in the first place. Tragically, Major Tilden died in the shooting, but his death became a catalyst for measures to be taken to curb the killings. Thereafter, an order was passed forbidding citizen patrols from carrying guns and even tightened regulations for soldiers using their weapons.

Virtually no incident during those few days was ever investigated in the aftermath. When all was said and done, sentries turned a blind eye to the deeds performed by their fellow patrolman and vigilante citizens, whether it was lawful or not.

Though the numerous stories make it seem like the city was practically lawless following the quake, for the most part, it was not. Truthfully, the strict order that was needed to get through the crisis was kept to, thanks mainly to a large and varied volunteer force of professionals that tirelessly patrolled the city. All in all, mass panic and major instances of crime were held at bay, and the city was prevented from descending into complete anarchy.

Chapter 8 – "Strangers in Our Own Streets"

"We were strangers in our own streets, refugees from our own houses."

—Henry A Lafler, Journalist

After fires had blazed across the city, the words Lafler expressed were felt by multitudes. Some half-crazed with fear, some stumbling about numbly, the suffering in the city was palpable. People struggled to find safety, medical assistance, or basic necessities. Some cried and called out for loved ones that were nowhere to be found.

Some "refugees" found help from kind strangers. Many of the affluent houses in the upper district had been initially spared destruction, so owners opened their homes and gathered up passing strangers who needed shelter and food. In one home, twenty refuges were allowed to sleep in the drawing room. The next morning, the owner took all that remained of her food stores—some flour and baking powder—and made breakfast for her hungry guests. But even this refuge would not provide a long-term place for safety. The fire was making its way into the neighborhood, and homeowners and refugees alike were forced to flee.

Despite the dynamite blasts used to slow or stop the fires, the movement of the conflagrations could not be wholly predicted. With many now homeless or fleeing fires that approached their neighborhoods, there were few places to find assured safety.

Thousands of people arrived at the ferry docks, many on foot, carrying what belongings they could and begging to be let onto the departing boats. Many had been forced to flee their homes without warning, so they had nothing with them and could not even afford the ten-cent fare to be taken across the bay. Those who had been able to pay the obscenely inflated prices (as much as $50) to be transported to the ferry by a driver were not guaranteed a chance to leave either.

From the ferry area, flames could be seen in the city all around, increasing the people's panic and urgency. G. A. Raymond, whose harrowing tale of escape was noted earlier, was one of the many who reached the ferry docks. He, like many others, believed that reaching the ferry would mean that they were saved. But upon arriving there, any hope for safety or comfort was soon shattered. Raymond described the scene as "bedlam, pandemonium, and hell rolled into one."

In his estimates, as many as ten thousand panicked people fought like wild animals to get on board the ferries Frantic survivors begged for safe passage and food while women fainted from thirst. People tore at each other, ripping the clothing from the backs of anyone in their way, and fear caused grown men to lose their reason. One man, who was rendered senseless from the chaos and anguish, beat his head on an iron pillar and shouted in agony, "The city must be saved!"

When the gates to the ferries were finally opened, further chaos ensued. The mad rush swept everyone within the crowd aboard the ferries, jamming people into every square inch of the boats. But as G. A. Raymond remarked, no one cared about the overcrowded conditions—there was only relief to be escaping the city.

Yet, as packed as the ferries were, not all were able to find space. Many more people remained on the dock, unable to board. As the last boat pulled away from the dock, frantic men and women made desperate attempts to jump aboard only to fall into the water, some possibly having jumped to their deaths.

Those who could not leave the city were compelled to find locales within it where the fire could not reach them. Without any source of shelter in the first few days and nights, both rich and poor, citizens and immigrants, were forced to camp out in the open within whatever safe zone they could reach. With the fires burning on the eastern part of the city, many migrated to the western side.

Some sought safety within the boundaries of the Presidio. Occupying 1,480 acres of land, the Presidio military installation was mostly open ground, containing few buildings or homes over its vast expanse. Though there was a chance fire would reach the forest within its areas, it was still a safer option than most.

Aside from the Presidio (which reached all the way to the Golden Gate Channel), many escaped to the open grounds of the nearby one-thousand-acre Golden Gate Park. From its sparsely populated surroundings down to the soft golden sand dunes that met the Pacific Ocean, the park became a safe haven to rest. It sat in a relatively peaceful juxtaposition to the fiery, charred ruins that many had fled.

Others sought a more macabre safety among the dead, camping out in graveyards and, where possible, sheltering in mausoleum-type vaults alongside the coffins of the deceased.

Smaller outdoor plazas and parks also served as a temporary refuge for those who reached them, though they may have felt somewhat less secure than in larger spaces like the Presidio or Golden Gate Park. Alta Plaza, sitting on the crest of a hill and taking up a relatively paltry area of four city blocks (twelve acres), was one such place. During the nights, refugees huddled together among their bundles of belongings, hellish fires burning brightly around them, turning the darkness to daylight. One man who spent a night in Alta Plaza recalled seeing firefighters retreat into the plaza throughout the night, dropping down breathless with exhaustion. There was little in the way of food or water to revive them save for some emergency food and a few buckets of water reserved specifically for the returning heroes. However, a sergeant carried something that practically amounted to gold at the time—one precious bottle of whisky, which he gave to the tired firemen.

While men defended the city from fires and crime, the women stepped up to do their part. They comforted and cared for the needs of others, especially those who had been separated from spouses or children in the initial chaos. They displayed their own courage, self-sacrifice, and compassion when others needed it most.

Jane Tingley, a well-known writer, was one such heroine. She recounted one particularly heartbreaking story of coming across a disheveled, half-naked woman in Golden Gate Park. The woman, her stare fixed on the water beyond, repeated in a trance-like chant, "Here I am, my pretties. Come here, come here." Compassionately taking her by the hand, Jane brought the woman down the hill to her husband, who was weeping. Explaining his wife's state, he told Jane, "She is calling our three little children. She thinks the sounds of the ocean waves are the voices of our lost darlings." Having become separated from their young children during the rush to flee the fire, the parents had been searching all over for them, taking no time for food or rest. Of everyone they saw, they forlornly asked the same question, "Have you seen anything of our lost babies?" Yet, Jane knew that it might be days before the pitiful parents would have an answer as to what became of their children.

Lost children were not the only urgent issue that arose amidst the crisis. Unfortunately, for a number of heavily pregnant women, their unborn children decided to come into the world with some of the worst possible timing. Among the parks, the dunes, and the Presidio, babies were born out in the open with sparse medical assistance or equipment. One wealthy city resident, with the help of an amateur midwife, even gave birth on the front lawn of her mansion while the family waited for the dynamite squad to come and blow up their stately home. The midwife, on seeing the newborn open its eyes, wryly remarked, "God sends earthquakes and babies, but He might, in His mercy, cut out sending them both together."

According to Jane Tingley, nine new lives were ushered into the world that day. Eight babies were recorded being born in Buena Vista Park, but scholars believe many others were born in various locations around the city. Sadly, the mortality rate of the new mothers and babies was high, with many dying in the places they sought refuge.

However, not all of the new births had a tragic ending. Tingley recalled the night when a soldier begged her to go help another woman. Without telling her what was happening, he simply pointed her to a hedge of bushes. When she walked into the brush, she saw a crudely constructed shelter made with a blanket. Inside the shelter lay a woman naked in the grass, clothes torn and scattered around her. It was immediately evident to Jane that the poor woman, all alone, was in labor. Sending someone to find a doctor, she was soon joined by two other women who came to help. Although no doctor could be found, a medical student was sent over to assist. Of the baby's arrival, Tingley wrote, "Under the best ministrations we could find, a new life was ushered into this hell, which, a few hours before, was the fairest among cities."

Though within the first two days after the quake, many within the city were able to find safety and some form of shelter from the fire, more pressing needs soon arose as the city began to hunger and thirst.

Chapter 9 – Sweet Relief and Labors of Mercy

Though it was apparent to city officials early on that measures needed to be taken to prevent a famine from compounding the problems the city faced, implementing these steps would be more difficult. For two days, not one supply of food (or anything for that matter) was able to come into the city.

At first, the soldiers did what they could to find even the most meager supplies to feed the hungry people gathered in the squares by commandeering bread from bakeries or using emergency reserves. Military stores had adequate supplies and were opened to citizens. But with no way of receiving news or communication that these stores were open to the public, most were ignorant of the existence of these provisions and could not take advantage of them. But soon thereafter, General Frederick Funston used the food stocks in the Presidio and sent rations out to the city to be distributed among the hungry.

As the fires raged, quick-thinking officers and soldiers had all foodstuffs and supplies from grocery stores that were in danger of burning conveyed to safer locations. In total, 390 stores had their contents saved, with that food going to feed refugees in the coming days. Stores that remained open quickly ran low on supplies. It wasn't long before fresh foods disappeared, with those in the city relying on crackers and canned foods to assuage their hunger. Those who were able to buy food had to do so at a premium, as many store owners doubled their prices despite the order against price gouging.

As soldiers began collecting carcasses of dead animals around the city, grotesque rumors arose that the military was using these to feed refugees. It was patently false, but given what was happening on the shores of Lake Merced, the story almost seemed plausible. Hungry refugees around the lake, becoming desperate for food, spotted live ducks and swans the city kept as decorations. But looking less like adornments and more like a meal, several men jumped into the lake and swam after the waterfowl. Within a short time, every duck had been cooked and eaten.

But it was obvious that 300,000 people could not be sustained on city ducks and rescued crackers. Without action, famine would rage quickly on the heels of the doused fires.

Even more urgent was the matter of finding fresh drinking water for the city, without which death was only a matter of a few days away. Full reservoirs teased the people with its water, yet their distance and difficulty in being reached prevented them from being a quick solution. Still, something had to be done, so wagons were mounted with barrels of water and driven through the park, with soldiers guarding the precious commodity against the thirsty citizens eager to ease their suffering. But with a one drink per person allowance, the quenching of thirst was short-lived.

With the danger of famine looming in the days after the quake, Mayor Schmitz gave orders for "supplies to be given to those in need." That would be no small feat. On the afternoon of the great quake, Mayor Schmitz had already known that the city government was ill-equipped to handle a crisis of that magnitude. That day, he quickly gathered the city's most able lawyers, leaders, and businessmen and created the now well-known Committee of Fifty, which included the mayor himself as chairman.[4]

In the days following the quake, the committee was tasked with distributing food to the city. Word of the disaster had spread across the state and country, including even the federal government.[5] Within days, food, medical supplies, and other necessities began pouring into the city from all over California and the rest of the country. Trains and steamer ships arrived laden with necessities sent by civil organizations as well as other military bases. But all these supplies needed to be received, transported, and stored before distribution.

In less than a week, the relief effort had become too overwhelming for the Committee of Fifty, and the mayor turned to the army for help. The quartermaster of the Presidio, Major Carroll Devol, was charged with receiving, transporting, and distributing supplies from the outpost. General Adolphus Greely was asked to handle the enormous job of fairly distributing food to the thousands of citizens who desperately depended on them.

At first, Greely was reluctant to accept the assignment and refused. The Committee of Fifty pressed him to reconsider, and eventually, he relented. Greely got to work setting up nine food depots around the city while the Presidio cared for the sixteen thousand refugees who sought help within its confines.[6] Even though there were supplies coming into the city, food and water were strictly rationed, with each person receiving three-quarters of a soldier's ration.

---

[4] The Committee of Fifty has also been referred to as the Citizen's Committee of Fifty and the Citizen's Relief Committee.

[5] Money was also sent from various relief organizations, with the US government taking the lead in appropriating $1,000,000 to relief funds.

[6] This number is based on army reports. The army also reported that 30,000 citizens were so destitute that they were completely dependent on the army for food and shelter. However, in total, 300,000 were fed at army food stations on April 30th alone.

At first, the need for food was so great that it went out to be distributed as fast as it came in, with little thought given to balanced allocation. As long as it was food, it was going out to the people. Despite little initial organization, by the end of the week, the danger of famine had passed.

While the regular army worked to stave off the famine, the Army Corp of Engineers took on the duties of supplying water to the city. With the city's main waterlines shattered, not only clean drinking water but also sanitation moved up the list of growing priorities. Dr. Marcus Herstein, a member of the Committee of Fifty, pointed out that if the water mains were broken, there was no doubt that the sewer system had been decimated as well. He predicted that they would soon find the city "covered with the stumps of open sewer pipes." The rats would have easy access to all parts of the city, with "the main sewers as boulevards." Open sewers and rats were a potential health and hygiene nightmare, and it was a new potential disaster the city could ill afford.

Among the list of priorities was also shelter, something desperately needed by refugees who had fled their homes with nothing more than the thin covering of clothes on their backs. Air temperatures were mild, and camping in the park may not have seemed to be the worst option, but as luck would have it, severe rains moved in on the days following the quake, compounding the suffering of those who had lost their homes. Two nights that week, pouring rains soaked the poor unfortunate souls living out in the open. Even those who had crude shelters set up found them to be wholly inadequate against the deluge-like rains. All those outside during the storms ended up shivering and soaked to the bone, increasing the urgency for shelters.

Making sure that everyone received the needed food, water, and shelter was logistically difficult with such a fluid situation. Many homeless, having no permanent location, moved around the city, making it difficult to figure out how and where to effectively organize and meet everyone's needs. Thus, boundary lines were set, and six districts were created, breaking the areas up into territories that troops could be assigned to care for. As this organizational effort began, it became apparent that reinforcements were needed. A plea to the War Department led to an additional 1,500 troops and 45 officers being dispatched to the city to help with the relief.

The initial hasty relief effort soon started to give way to more organized provisions. One hundred thirty-five carpenters set to work building shelters. Eight large temporary shed-like structures were put up in Golden Gate Park, where a large bulk of the refugees camped. Thousands without tents were able to be housed in these, and though they were pretty rudimentary, they were much more comfortable than living in the open. As more structures were built, the designs also improved in small ways. Builders divided them into compartments, each with its own outside entrance. They were able to reasonably house a family and give them a bit of blessed privacy.

The military also issued a total of twenty-five thousand tents— some common tents but the majority being shelter tents—and these were also set up in Golden Gate Park, as well as other parks and open areas. More scattered tents in outlying areas were also systematically gathered into the camp system. Each camp had a number, and even the tents within were given numbers, a sort of temporary address that made conditions just a little homier.

Day by day, the camps continued to grow into completed systems. Lumber from a loaded schooner in the bay was commandeered and brought to the Engineer Corps to create tent floors, letting refugees get off the dirt and live in more comfortable conditions.

Once the shelters were up, the work did not end there. The camps, as organized as they became, were not like city neighborhoods with privately owned homes. They could not be left to administer themselves. Each camp had a military officer in charge of it with an army surgeon on-site responsible for medical needs as well as sanitation. Every camp was also assigned a Red Cross worker to deal with registering "residents," a process put in place to help organize the logistics of food, clothes, and other necessities each person or family would need.

While the camp system was being established, it was obvious to authorities that the food receiving and delivery system needed work. Major C. R. Krauthoff of the Subsistence Department had the unenviable task of smoothing out and perfecting that system. He would shortly devise a delivery system for food depots and relief camps. This system was set up in a way that ensured food supplies were more evenly distributed so that one camp didn't end up with all of the flour supplies and another with nothing but ham.

An abundance of water was also now being supplied to the camps. But with no water filtration or treatment system, they had to create a new one. So, the general hospital in each camp developed bacteria cultures that purified the water and rendered it fit for human consumption. Now, refugees not only had enough water to drink, but they could also bathe and wash. The camp even had a laundry service, which was sorely needed after days in the soot and dirt.

An interesting aspect of camp life had to do with social and cultural differences. Many who found themselves under a canvas in the dirt had just days before enjoyed the luxury of being served by butlers in their immaculate mansions. Now, the forces of nature had leveled the playing field for many. Both rich and poor, citizens and immigrants, suffered the same deprivations and lived under the same exact conditions for the first time in their lives. Tensions, differences in lifestyles, and differing backgrounds made it inevitable that incidents of rowdiness would break out as people trampled on the rights of others and showed disregard for commonly held decencies.

The closeness of camp life also gave rise to another inevitable problem—the easy spread of disease. However, the military's sanitation efforts were somewhat rewarded in this aspect. Though there were reported cases of typhoid fever and smallpox, there were no outbreaks on an epidemic level.

By the end of April, relief efforts were well in hand, with 300,000 people being cared for by authorities. The work wouldn't be over, though. There would be a massive effort to clean up and rebuild. And that cleanup effort would include the grim task of finding and burying the dead.

The bodies that had not been burned in the fire needed to be cared for quickly. Though the search and recovery started while the flames still raged, it would continue into the days after.

Taking care of the dead was perhaps the most heartbreaking and difficult of tasks. It was truly a labor of mercy, and not all did so willingly. Soldiers, police, and firemen were needed for other work, so citizens were drafted to help. Those who objected quickly found out that they did not have a choice in the matter, some staring down the barrel of a soldier's gun. Troops needed every capable male to pitch in, and they would not stand for dissension.

At first, bodies were conveyed to city squares, which served as temporary public morgues, a gruesome sight for those who sought safety from the fires. Those seeking sanctuary in places like Mechanics' Pavilion and Portsmouth Square would be further traumatized by the nearness of as many as twenty or thirty corpses laid together in the grass.

When fires began to threaten those areas, the necessity for quick burials arose so that the bodies were not lost to the flames. Other corpses were transported to the Presidio. But that required additional vehicles and drivers than soldiers had available. So, passing vehicles were pressed into service as sort of temporary hearses.

When the bodies began to pile up in the Presidio and other areas, they became a health hazard and required quick burials. A temporary cemetery was opened, and the grueling work of digging graves by hand was left both to those who did so voluntarily and those who were forcibly compelled. Rich and working class alike picked up spades and labored through the dirt, side by side. Once the graves were dug, the men lowered the bodies into the earth. There was no time for individual burials, so several bodies were placed into each grave.

Sadly, many of the dead were never identified and went to their final resting place unknown. Names of those who could be identified were written down, and those whose names were unknown had descriptions written of them in hopes their loved ones might be able to recognize them. Many went without the comfort of seeing their loved ones have a proper funeral.

Those who were buried with their loved ones present created a pitiable scene. Especially so was one young girl whose father, her only relative, died in the earthquake. As the body was brought from place to place, she followed until it finally came to rest in the Presidio. She watched as her father was buried at the outpost, weeping as other women tried to comfort her. Others wept for their loved ones alongside her, many kneeling on the ground as a Catholic priest performed funeral services throughout the day.

Chapter 10 – Rising from the Ashes

In the days and weeks that followed the great disaster, San Francisco underwent dramatic changes—even in less obvious ways. Many left the city during and after the crisis and didn't return, but those who stayed felt and displayed extraordinary comradery. Personal conflicts were put aside, racial barriers were broken down and forgotten, and social distinctions no longer mattered—everyone was on a level playing field.

For weeks after the disaster, the mayor upheld the order that no fires could be lit inside houses. Those with houses still standing brought stoves outside and cooked on sidewalks and in the streets. Those who previously had servants to prepare meals now had to fend for themselves, and even the most well-heeled and highly educated women prepared meals under the sky.

For those that remained in the camps for the months and years following the earthquake, they began to establish regular routines, their lives taking on a somewhat normal tone with gatherings in dining halls and children playing with newfound friends. The city had union carpenters build cottages (5,300 in total), dubbed "earthquake shacks," for the newly homeless, which allowed the people to slowly move out of tents and into their new lives.

Marriages around the city skyrocketed as women were left homeless by the disaster, now turning to their fiancés to give them a home. New life continued to emerge, even in unlikely places—a baby was born behind some screens on the sidewalk in front of his parents' mansion, and in the same night, the next block over, a litter of kittens was born to a lost cat.

Dr. Herstein's fears regarding rats and the spread of disease were legitimate, as bubonic plague broke out in the city and not just among the homeless or immigrant communities. In total, there were 160 cases confirmed, and 14 died in one month.

Many praised the mayor, some raising him to near hero status after his handling of the crisis. Even regular critics like those at the *Bulletin* suspended its critical comments about the mayor in the weeks that followed. They were not the only ones to put aside political rivalries in the interest of rebuilding. As the *Bulletin* noted, "the fire burned out old enmities" between political factions, and the paper remained committed to cooperating "with the men who are laying the foundations of the new San Francisco."

Those men in charge of the rebuilding formed a new city committee. The Committee of Fifty was disbanded and replaced with the Committee of Forty on the Reconstruction of San Francisco, headed by Abraham "Boss" Ruef. One of the reconstruction efforts the city underwent involved the heavily damaged water supply system. From this, a better system arose, and construction of the city's Auxiliary Water Supply System—the largest high-pressure water distribution system ever built—was underway.

Regarding the changes the city underwent and would continue to undergo, author and journalist William Henry Owen mused, "Old San Francisco is dead...It is as though a pretty, frivolous woman has passed through a great tragedy. She survives, but she is sobered and different. If it rises out of the ashes, it must be a modern city." And arise from the ashes it did.

Conclusion

The great earthquake of 1906 was so intense that it was picked up by seismographs around the world, such as in Tokyo, Moscow, Berlin, Cape Town, and London. According to US Army reports at the time, there were 498 deaths in San Francisco; however, later reports by the National Oceanic and Atmospheric Agency (NOAA) estimate it could have been more like 700 to 800 (though, by some calculations, even those numbers underestimate the casualties San Francisco endured).

Though her damage was severe, San Francisco was not the only city that suffered. It is estimated that there were more than three thousand deaths caused directly or indirectly by the earthquake, including the more than one hundred people who died when the walls of Agnews State Asylum crumbled atop them.

Twenty-eight thousand buildings and around five hundred city blocks (4.7 square miles) were destroyed, leaving 225,000 people homeless and causing over $400 million in damages, making it one of the costliest and deadliest earthquakes in US history.[7]

---

[7] Today that would equate to around $8.2 billion.

Here's another book by Captivating History that you might like

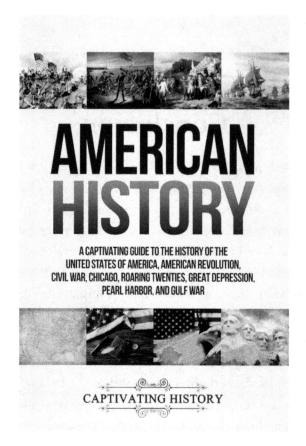

Free Bonus from Captivating History
(Available for a Limited time)

Hi History Lovers!

Now you have a chance to join our exclusive history list so you can get your first history ebook for free as well as discounts and a potential to get more history books for free! Simply visit the link below to join.

Captivatinghistory.com/ebook

Also, make sure to follow us on Facebook, Twitter and Youtube by searching for Captivating History.

References

Anderson, Michael. Frederick Funston: The Man Who Saved San Francisco.

www.parks.ca.gov/.

Bean, Walton (1974). Boss Ruef's San Francisco: The Story of the Union Labor Party, Big Business, and the Graft Prosecution. Berkeley: University of California Press. https://archive.org/details/bossruefssanfran00bean/page/122/mode/2 up.

Bronson, William (2014). The Earth Shook, The Sky Burned: A Photographic Record of the 1906 San Francisco Earthquake and Fire. Edition:100th. Publisher: Chronicle Books LLC.

Death of Fire Chief Engineer Dennis T. Sullivan. Virtual Museum of the City of San Francisco. Archived from the original on 2013-06-17. Retrieved 2021-3-10. http://www.sfmuseum.net/hist10/dtsullivan.html.

Dr. William Ellsworth Wallace, R.R. (ed.). The San Andreas Fault System. California, USGS Professional Paper 1515, Denver, CO, 283 pp., paperback, 1990.

Ellsworth, W.L., 1990, Earthquake history, 1769-1989, chap. 6 of Wallace, R.E., ed., The San Andreas Fault System, California: U.S.

Geological Survey Professional Paper 1515, p. 152-187. The Great 1906 San Francisco Earthquake *https://earthquake.usgs.gov/earthquakes/events/1906calif/18april/.*

Fradkin, Philip L., *The Great Earthquake and Firestorms of 1906, Archived June 9, 2007, at the Wayback Machine.*

History of the Presidio. www.presidio.gov/visit/history-of-the-presidio.

Lomax, A., (2005), A Reanalysis of the Hypocentral Location and Related Observations for the Great 1906 California Earthquake, *Bull. Seism. Soc. Am.,* 95, 861-877.

National Park Service, *From Presidio of San Francisco*

National Park Service; Agnews Insane Asylum www.nps.gov/places/agnews-insane-asylum.htm.

Schulz, Sandra S.; Wallace, Robert E. *The San Andreas Fault.* https:pubs.usgs.gov/.

Strobridge, William, *Soldiers in the Streets.* The Pacific Historian 22.1 (Spring 1978): 4

Thatcher, Wayne (December 10, 1975). *Strain accumulation and release mechanism of the 1906 San Francisco Earthquake. Journal of Geophysical Research.* 80 (35): 4862–4872. Bibcode:1975JGR....80.4862T..

Thomas S. Duke (1910) *Synopsis of the San Francisco Police and Municipal records of the Greatest Catastrophe in American History.* Published with Approval of the Honorable Board of Police Commissioners of San Francisco 1910

Thomas, Gordon; Morgan Witts, Max (1933, 1971) *The San Francisco Earthquake.* New York, Stein and Day

https://archive.org/details/sanfranciscoeart00thom/page/56/mode/2up.

USGS, *Casualties and damage after the 1906 Earthquake, United States Geological Survey.*
https://earthquake.usgs.gov/earthquakes/events/1906calif/18april/casualties.php.

Wallace, Gregory (2014) *The 10 Most Expensive U.S. Earthquakes.*
https://money.cnn.com/2014/08/24/news/economy/earthquakes-10-most-expensive/index.html.

Altman, Linda Jacobs. *The California Gold Rush in American History.* Enslow Publishers, 1997.

Caughey, John Walton and W. R. Cameron. *The California Gold Rush.* University of California Press, 1975.

"Graphs Showing Miners' Wages and Value of Gold Production, 1848-1860 · SHEC: Resources for Teachers." *Social History for Every Classroom,* shec.ashp.cuny.edu/items/show/1738.

Marks, Paula Mitchell. *Precious Dust: The American Gold Rush Era, 1848-1900.* W. Morrow, 1994.

Morison, Samuel Eliot. *The Oxford History of the American People.* Oxford University Press, 1965.

Sonneborn, Liz. *The California Gold Rush: Transforming the American West.* Chelsea House Publishers, 2009.

Stanley, Jerry. *Digger: The Tragic Fate of the California Indians from the Missions to the Gold Rush.* Crown Publishers, Inc., 1997.

White, Stewart Edward. *The Forty-Niners: A Chronicle of the California Trail and El Dorado.* Yale Univ. Press, 1921.

Alaska Public Land Information Centers. "How Close Is Alaska to Russia?" Your Guide to Experiencing Alaska's Public Lands. July 05, 2017. Accessed February 20, 2021.
https://www.alaskacenters.gov/faqs-people-often-ask/how-close-alaska-russia.

Bacich, Damian, Dr. "Timeline: European Exploration and Settlement of California." The California Frontier Project. June 01, 2018. Accessed February 24, 2021. https://www.californiafrontier.net/timeline-european-exploration-settlement/.

Bacich, Damian, Dr. "Juan Bautista De Anza: Son of the Frontier." The California Frontier Project. September 30, 2020. Accessed February 24, 2021. https://www.californiafrontier.net/juan-bautista-de-anza-son-of-the-frontier/.

Britannica, The Editors of Encyclopedia. "Pomo." Encyclopedia Britannica. June 10, 2019. Accessed February 23, 2021. https://www.britannica.com/topic/Pomo-people.

Britannica, The Editors of Encyclopedia. "Chumash." Encyclopedia Britannica. May 24, 2019. Accessed February 23, 2021. https://www.britannica.com/topic/Chumash.

Britannica, The Editors of Encyclopedia. "Gold Rush." Encyclopedia Britannica. October 16, 2019. Accessed February 24, 2021. https://www.britannica.com/event/gold-rush.

Britannica, The Editors of Encyclopedia. "Hollywood." Encyclopedia Britannica. November 19, 2019. Accessed February 25, 2021. https://www.britannica.com/place/Hollywood-California.

Britannica, The Editors of Encyclopedia. "Miwok." Encyclopedia Britannica. April 8, 2020. Accessed February 23, 2021. https://www.britannica.com/topic/Miwok.

Britannica, The Editors of Encyclopedia. "Juan Rodríguez Cabrillo." Encyclopedia Britannica. March 9, 2020. Accessed February 23, 2021. https://www.britannica.com/biography/Juan-Rodriguez-Cabrillo.

Britannica, The Editors of Encyclopedia. "San Diego." Encyclopedia Britannica. May 7, 2020. Accessed February 24, 2021. https://www.britannica.com/place/San-Diego-California.

Britannica, The Editors of Encyclopedia. "St. Junípero Serra." Encyclopedia Britannica. November 20, 2020. Accessed February 24, 2021. https://www.britannica.com/biography/Saint-Junipero-Serra.

Britannica, The Editors of Encyclopedia. "Mexican-American War." Encyclopedia Britannica. November 10, 2020. Accessed February 24, 2021. https://www.britannica.com/event/Mexican-American-War.

Britannica, The Editors of Encyclopedia. "Bear Flag Revolt." Encyclopedia Britannica. February 14, 2020. Accessed February 24, 2021. https://www.britannica.com/event/Bear-Flag-Revolt.

Britannica, The Editors of Encyclopedia. "California Gold Rush." Encyclopedia Britannica. May 27, 2020. Accessed February 24, 2021. https://www.britannica.com/topic/California-Gold-Rush.

Britannica, The Editors of Encyclopedia. "San Francisco Earthquake of 1906." Encyclopedia Britannica. May 12, 2020. Accessed February 25, 2021. https://www.britannica.com/event/San-Francisco-earthquake-of-1906.

Britannica, The Editors of Encyclopedia. "Juan Ponce De León." Encyclopedia Britannica. January 01, 2021. Accessed February 24, 2021.

https://www.britannica.com/biography/Juan-Ponce-de-Leon.

Britannica, The Editors of Encyclopedia. "John Sutter." Encyclopedia Britannica. February 12, 2021. Accessed February 24, 2021. https://www.britannica.com/biography/John-Sutter.

California Military History. "Proclamation of the Bear Flag Revolt." The Mexican War and California. June 23, 2017. Accessed February 24, 2021.

http://www.militarymuseum.org/BearFlagRevolt.html.

California Native American Heritage Commission. "Short Overview of California Indian History." California Indian History – California Native American Heritage Commission. 2021. Accessed February 18, 2021. http://nahc.ca.gov/resources/california-indian-history/.

California State Capitol Museum. "Called to Action: California's Role in WW2."

California Transformed. 2016. Accessed February 26, 2021.

http://www.capitolmuseum.ca.gov/special/ww2/introduction/california-transformed.

California State Parks. "Hernando de Alarcón Expedition." State of California. 2021.

Accessed February 24, 2021. https://ohp.parks.ca.gov/ListedResources/Detail/568.

California State University. "Mexican California: The Heyday of the Ranchos." California History Online | The First Californians. 2021. Accessed February 24, 2021. http://www.csun.edu/~sg4002/courses/417/readings/mexican.pdf.

California State University. "The Great Depression: California in the Thirties." CSUN. 2021. Accessed February 25, 2021.

http://www.csun.edu/~sg4002/courses/417/readings/depression.pdf.

Caryl-Sue, National Geographic Society. "Columbus Makes Landfall in the Caribbean." National Geographic Society. September 6, 2020. Accessed February 24, 2021. https://www.nationalgeographic.org/thisday/oct12/columbus-makes-landfall-caribbean/.

De Portola Middle. "Who Is Gaspar de Portola?" We've Got History. 2021. Accessed February 24, 2021.

https://deportola.sandiegounified.org/about_us/who_is_gaspar_de_portola.

Defense Language Institute Foreign Language Center. "History of the Presidio of

Monterey." DLIFLC. 2021. Accessed February 24, 2021.

https://www.dliflc.edu/about/command-history/online-exhibit-history-of-the-presidio-of-monterey/.

Desert USA and Digital West Media, Inc. "Juan Bautista De Anza." Desert USA. 2020. Accessed February 24, 2021. https://www.desertusa.com/desert-people/juan-bautista-de-anza.html.

Fen Montaigne, Jennie Rothenberg Gritz. "The Story of How Humans Came to the Americas Is Constantly Evolving." Smithsonian.com. Jan. & Feb. 2020. Accessed February 18, 2021. https://www.smithsonianmag.com/science-nature/how-humans-came-to-americas-180973739/.

Frommer's. "History in California." Frommer's. 2021. Accessed February 26, 2021.

https://www.frommers.com/destinations/california/in-depth/history.

Greshko, Michael. "Humans in California 130,000 Years Ago? Get the Facts." Culture. April 26, 2017. Accessed February 18, 2021.

https://www.nationalgeographic.com/culture/article/mastodons-americas-peopling-migrations-archaeology-science.

History.com Editors. "Vasco Núñez De Balboa." History.com. August 21, 2018. Accessed February 24, 2021. https://www.history.com/topics/exploration/vasco-nunez-de-balboa.

History.com Editors. "Hollywood." History.com. March 27, 2018. Accessed February 25, 2021. https://www.history.com/topics/roaring-twenties/hollywood.

History.com Editors. "California Becomes the 31st State in Record Time." A&E Television Networks. September 9, 2020. Accessed February 24, 2021. https://www.history.com/this-day-in-history/california-becomes-the-31st-state-in-record-time.

Inda, Estella. "What's in a Name—California." San Jose Public Library. September 01, 2018. Accessed February 23, 2021. https://www.sjpl.org/blog/whats-name-california.

Innes, Ralph Hammond. "Hernán Cortés." Encyclopedia Britannica. January 07, 2021. Accessed February 24, 2021. https://www.britannica.com/biography/Hernan-Cortes.

Keen, Benjamin. "Vasco Núñez De Balboa." Encyclopedia Britannica. January 08, 2021. Accessed February 24, 2021. https://www.britannica.com/biography/Vasco-Nunez-de-Balboa.

Lonely Planet. "History of California." Lonely Planet. 2021. Accessed February 26, 2021. https://www.lonelyplanet.com/usa/california/history#110261.

Los Angeles Almanac. "Pio Pico - Last Governor of Mexican California." Los Angeles Almanac. 2021. Accessed February 24, 2021.

http://www.laalmanac.com/history/hi05s.php.

MacroTrends. "California Population 1900–2020." MacroTrends. 2021. Accessed February 26, 2021. https://www.macrotrends.net/states/california/population.

Martha Heasley Cox Center for Steinbeck Studies. "1920 to 1930: A Period of Extremes." 1920 to 1930 | Steinbeck in the Schools | San Jose State University. October 25, 2016. Accessed February 26, 2021.

https://sits.sjsu.edu/context/historical/hist_context_1920s/index.html
.

Martha Heasley Cox Center for Steinbeck Studies. "1950–1960 Laying the Foundation." Steinbeck in the Schools | San Jose State University. October 25, 2016. Accessed February 26, 2021. https://sits.sjsu.edu/context/historical/hist_context_1950s/index.html
.

Martha Heasley Cox Center for Steinbeck Studies. "World War II Homefront." Steinbeck in the Schools | San Jose State University. October 25, 2016. Accessed February 26, 2021. https://sits.sjsu.edu/context/historical/hist_context_1940s_homefront/index.html.

McNamee, Gregory Lewis, and Neil Morgan. "California." Encyclopedia Britannica. February 04, 2021. Accessed February 24, 2021.

https://www.britannica.com/place/California-state.

National Historic Trail. "Juan Bautista De Anza." Welcome to the Anza Historic Trail. 2021. Accessed February 24, 2021. http://www.anzahistorictrail.org/.

National Park Service U.S Department of the Interior. "The Bering Land Bridge Theory." National Parks Service. January 29, 2021. Accessed February 20, 2021. https://www.nps.gov/bela/learn/historyculture/the-bering-land-bridge-theory.htm.

National Parks Service. "Early History of the California Coast." National Parks Service. Accessed February 23, 2021. https://www.nps.gov/nr/travel/ca/intro.htm#:~:text=On September 28, 1542, Juan,land for thousands of years.

New World Encyclopedia. "Atsugewi." Atsugewi - New World Encyclopedia. April 26,

2016. Accessed February 21, 2021.

https://www.newworldencyclopedia.org/entry/Atsugewi.

New World Encyclopedia. "Modoc People." Modoc People - New World Encyclopedia. October 12, 2018. Accessed February 21, 2021.

https://www.newworldencyclopedia.org/entry/Modoc_people.

New World Encyclopedia. "Achomawi." Achomawi - New World Encyclopedia. November 3, 2019. Accessed February 21, 2021. https://www.newworldencyclopedia.org/entry/Achomawi.

O'Brien, Cynthia, and Jamie Kiffel Alcheh. "Native People of California." History. February 16, 2021. Accessed February 18, 2021. https://kids.nationalgeographic.com/history/article/native-people-of-california.

Oakland Museum of California. "Early Statehood: 1850–1880s: Federal Indian Policy & the Modoc War." Picture This. 2021. Accessed February 25, 2021. http://picturethis.museumca.org/timeline/early-statehood-1850-1880s/modoc-war/info.

Oakland Museum of California. "Progressive Era: 1890–1920s: Immigration Period of Restrictions." Picture This. 2021. Accessed February 25, 2021. http://picturethis.museumca.org/timeline/progressive-era-1890-1920s/immigration-period-restrictions/info.

Oakland Museum of California. "Early Statehood: 1850–1880s: Women's Rights." Picture This. 2021. Accessed February 25, 2021. http://picturethis.museumca.org/timeline/early-statehood-1850-1880s/womens-rights/info.

Oakland Museum of California. "Progressive Era: 1890–1920s: Effects of 1906 Earthquake." Picture This. 2021. Accessed February 25, 2021. http://picturethis.museumca.org/timeline/progressive-era-1890-1920s/effects-1906-earthquake/info.

Oakland Museum of California. "Depression Era: 1930s: Depression." Picture This. 2021. Accessed February 26, 2021. http://picturethis.museumca.org/timeline/depression-era-1930s/depression/info.

Oakland Museum of California. "Depression Era: 1930s: 'Bloody Thursday' & Other Labor Strikes." Picture This. 2021. Accessed February 26, 2021. http://picturethis.museumca.org/timeline/depression-era-1930s/political-protest/info.

Pastron, Otto. "California in WW1 - Then." United States Foundation for the Commemoration of the World Wars. 2021. Accessed February 26, 2021. https://www.worldwar1centennial.org/index.php/california-in-ww1-then.html.

PBS. "The West - Junipero Serra." Public Broadcasting Service. 2001. Accessed February 24, 2021. https://www.pbs.org/weta/thewest/people/s_z/serra.htm.

PBS American Experience. "Transcontinental Railroad Timeline." PBS. 2021. Accessed February 24, 2021. https://www.pbs.org/wgbh/americanexperience/features/tcrr-timeline/.

PBS American Experience. "Workers of the Central and Union Pacific Railroad." PBS. 2021. Accessed February 24, 2021.

https://www.pbs.org/wgbh/americanexperience/features/tcrr-workers-central-union-pacific-railroad/.

Prine, Paul E., and Lowell John Bean. "California Indian." Encyclopedia Britannica. May

29, 2019. Accessed February 18, 2021. https://www.britannica.com/topic/California-Indian.

San Diego History Center. "Sebastián Vizcaíno." San Diego History Center: San Diego, CA: Our City, Our Story. 2021. Accessed February 24, 2021.

https://sandiegohistory.org/archives/biographysubject/vizcaino/.

San Diego Tourism Authority. "History: San Diego's 250th Anniversary." History. November 21, 2019. Accessed February 24, 2021. https://sandiego250.com/history/.

Santa Cruz Museum of Natural History. "Virtual Exhibit: First Peoples of California." Santa Cruz Museum of Natural History. November 03, 2020. Accessed February 18, 2021. https://www.santacruzmuseum.org/first-peoples-of-california-virtual-exhibit/.

Smithsonian National Postal Museum. "Settlement of California." Settlement of California | National Postal Museum. 2021. Accessed February 24, 2021.

https://postalmuseum.si.edu/exhibition/celebrating-hispanic-heritage-growth-settlement-of-the-southwest/settlement-of-california.

Starr, Kevin. *California: A History.* Modern Library, 2007.

State of California. "The Civil War in California." California Department of Parks and Recreation. 2021. Accessed February 24, 2021.

https://www.parks.ca.gov/?page_id=26775.

Steen, Francis F. "Local California Chronology 2: The First European Contact." 2. The First European Contact. March 31, 2002. Accessed February 24, 2021.

http://cogweb.ucla.edu/Chumash/California_First_Europeans.html.

The American Battlefield Trust. "10 Facts: California during the Civil War." American Battlefield Trust. May 31, 2018. Accessed February 24, 2021. https://www.battlefields.org/learn/articles/10-facts-california-during-civil-war.

The American Oil & Gas Historical Society. "First California Oil Wells." American Oil & Gas Historical Society. September 07, 2020. Accessed February 25, 2021. https://www.aoghs.org/petroleum-pioneers/first-california-oil-well/.

The California Historical Society. "Meanwhile out West: Colonizing California, 1769–1821." California Historical Society. June 27, 2019. Accessed February 24, 2021. https://californiahistoricalsociety.org/exhibitions/meanwhile-out-west-colonizing-california-1769-1821/.

The Library of Congress. "The First Peoples of California." California as I Saw It: First-Person Narratives of California's Early Years, 1849 to 1900. 2021. Accessed February 18, 2021. https://www.loc.gov/collections/california-first-person-narratives/articles-and-essays/early-california-history/first-peoples-of-california/.

The Library of Congress. "Spanish California." California as I Saw It: First-Person Narratives of California's Early Years, 1849 to 1900. 2021. Accessed February 23, 2021. https://www.loc.gov/collections/california-first-person-narratives/articles-and-essays/early-california-history/spanish-california/.

The Library of Congress. "Mexican California: Early California History: An Overview: Articles and Essays." California as I Saw It: First-Person Narratives of California's Early Years, 1849-1900. 2021. Accessed February 24, 2021.

https://www.loc.gov/collections/california-first-person-narratives/articles-and-essays/early-california-history/mexican-california/.

The Library of Congress. "The United States and California." California as I Saw It: First-Person Narratives of California's Early Years, 1849 to 1900. 2021. Accessed February 24, 2021. https://www.loc.gov/collections/california-first-person-narratives/articles-and-essays/early-california-history/united-states-and-california/.

The Library of Congress. "The Discovery of Gold." The Library of Congress. 2021. Accessed February 25, 2021. https://www.loc.gov/collections/california-first-person-narratives/articles-and-essays/early-california-history/discovery-of-gold/.

The Library of Congress. "The Mines." The Library of Congress. 2021. Accessed February 24, 2021. https://www.loc.gov/collections/california-first-person-narratives/articles-and-essays/early-california-history/mines/.

The Library of Congress. "Government and Law." The Library of Congress. 2021. Accessed February 24, 2021. https://www.loc.gov/collections/california-first-person-narratives/articles-and-essays/early-california-history/government-and-law/.

The Library of Congress. "From Gold Rush to Golden State." The Library of Congress. 2021. Accessed February 24, 2021. https://www.loc.gov/collections/california-first-person-narratives/articles-and-essays/early-california-history/from-gold-rush-to-golden-state/.

The Library of Congress. "California: Magnet for Tourists and Home Buyers." The Library of Congress. 2021. Accessed February 25, 2021. https://www.loc.gov/collections/california-first-person-narratives/articles-and-essays/early-california-history/magnet-for-tourists-and-home-buyers/.

The Library of Congress. "Other Californians." The Library of Congress. 2021. Accessed February 25, 2021. https://www.loc.gov/collections/california-first-person-narratives/articles-and-essays/early-california-history/other-californians/.

The Library of Congress. "The Turn of the Century in California." The Library of Congress. 2021. Accessed February 25, 2021. https://www.loc.gov/collections/california-first-person-narratives/articles-and-essays/early-california-history/turn-of-the-century-in-california/.

The National Parks Service. "Five Views: An Ethnic Historic Site Survey for California (Japanese Americans)." U.S. Department of the Interior. November 17, 2004. Accessed February 26, 2021. https://www.nps.gov/parkhistory/online_books/5views/5views4b.htm.

The National Parks Service. "National Park Service." National Parks Service. March 22, 2005. Accessed February 24, 2021.

https://www.nps.gov/parkhistory/online_books/explorers/sitee4.htm.

The National Parks Service. "California's Role in the Civil War." U.S. Department of the Interior. May 13, 2020. Accessed February 24, 2021.

https://www.nps.gov/goga/learn/historyculture/california-in-civil-war.htm.

The National Parks Service. "San Diego Mission Church (San Diego De Alcala)—Early History of the California Coast—A National Register of Historic Places Travel Itinerary." National Parks Service. 2021. Accessed February 24, 2021.

https://www.nps.gov/nr/travel/ca/ca3.htm.

U.S. Geological Survey. "The Great 1906 San Francisco Earthquake." U.S. Geological Survey. 2021. Accessed February 25, 2021.

https://earthquake.usgs.gov/earthquakes/events/1906calif/18april/.

Union Pacific. "Union Pacific History and Chronologies." Union Pacific. 2021. Accessed February 24, 2021. https://www.up.com/heritage/history/.

University of California. "San Francisco General Strike." Calisphere. 2005. Accessed February 25, 2021. https://calisphere.org/exhibitions/31/san-francisco-general-strike/.

University of Minnesota Libraries. "Sea Otter." The University of Minnesota Libraries. 2021. Accessed February 24, 2021. https://www.lib.umn.edu/bell/tradeproducts/seaotter.

University of Virginia. "'Free Labor' Ideology in the North." Virginia Center for Digital History. 2005. Accessed February 24, 2021.

http://www.vcdh.virginia.edu/solguide/VUS06/essay06c.html.